Already Whole

90 DEVOTIONS FOR BEING AT HOME IN THE BODY GOD GAVE YOU

ELLEN WILDMAN

Our Daily Bread
Publishing.

Requests for permission to quote from this book should be directed to: Permissions Department, Our Daily Bread Publishing, PO Box 3566, Grand Rapids, MI 49501; or contact us by email at permissionsdept@odbm.org.

Scripture quotations, unless otherwise indicated, are taken from the *Holy Bible*, New Living Translation, copyright © 1996, 2004, 2015 by Tyndale House Foundation. Used by permission of Tyndale House Publishers, Carol Stream, Illinois 60188. All rights reserved.

Scripture quotation marked CSB are taken from the Christian Standard Bible®, Copyright © 2017 by Holman Bible Publishers. Used by permission. Christian Standard Bible® and CSB® are federally registered trademarks of Holman Bible Publishers.

Scripture quotations marked ESV are taken from the ESV® Bible (The Holy Bible, English Standard Version®), copyright © 2001 by Crossway, a publishing ministry of Good News Publishers. Used by permission. All rights reserved.

Scripture quotations marked NIV are taken from the Holy Bible, New International Version®, NIV®. Copyright © 1973, 1978, 1984, 2011 by Biblica, Inc.™ Used by permission of Zondervan. All rights reserved worldwide. www.zondervan.com.

Interior design by Michael J. Williams

ISBN: 978-1-64070-397-1

Library of Congress Cataloging-in-Publication Data Available

Printed in China
25 26 27 28 29 30 31 32 / 8 7 6 5 4 3 2 1

Contents

Affirmations for the Journey

1. Reflecting God is an essential part of who I am. I am made in His image—His living, breathing handiwork.

2. Taking care of my body—physically, emotionally, and mentally—honors God and helps me to be more at home in the body God gave me.

3. When I look for God in others, I will naturally see beyond competition and comparison.

4. I am made in God's image, He designed my body, and He blessed it.

5. He said His creation was "very good" (Genesis 1:31). My body is good. Their body is good.

6. When I find myself struggling with the truth that my body is good, created in the perfect image of God, I hold on to God as a sustainer, a faithful presence that banishes shame.

7. This self-love journey isn't a quick fix, but a worthy pursuit of the wholeness God desires for me.

8. My worth is not determined by my weight. I am fearfully and wonderfully made, cherished by my Creator. My value is eternal, rooted in His love for me.

9. I am allowed to exist without apology and to show up just as I am.

10. The impossible ideals I have set for my body and myself will not bring me meaning. Instead, I choose to release those fruitless standards and look to God to define what a healthy and rewarding life means to me.

Hey Reader,

I'm so glad this book has made its way into your hands. As someone who has struggled with body image for most of my life, I know what it's like to have a complicated relationship with your body. I also know what it's like to find abundant freedom in fully accepting your body as created "very good" by God (Genesis 1:31). I wrote *Already Whole* because I want others to experience that same freedom, love, and care toward their body that I have found. It's my desire that the following devotions ease your inner critic, refresh your weary mind, and help you feel even just a little more at home in your body. I want you to know that your body is not a problem to be solved so you can finally enjoy life. Instead, it is a unique and intentional creation of Him, His living, breathing handiwork on display. God knew what body shape you would have, and He blessed it.

And just a heads up—this book is primarily written for those who call themselves Christians. If you aren't there yet, you can still find powerful truths within these pages, but you won't find the content as readily applicable. As you read this devotional, each day will end with an affirmation called "Embracing Wholeness." This is meant to serve as a daily encouragement and application, reminding you each and every day that you can embrace your inherent worth as God's creation here and now. This truth does not change. Repeat this affirmation to yourself, put it on a sticky note on your bathroom mirror, write it on an index card on your dashboard. Even if you don't believe every affirmation fully, there is power in repeating truth to yourself as you heal, grow, and change.

Your pathway to self-love will likely be one full of ups and downs, as mine has been. When you find yourself struggling with the truth that your body is good, part of your beautiful being that is created in the perfect image of God, may you hold on to God as a sustainer, His faithful presence banishing shame, even body shame. As you embark on this journey to greater self-acceptance, take comfort in knowing that God is with you every step of the way. He has never left you, and He won't start now.

Your body matters!

Ellen

Ellen Wildman

Connect with me on Instagram @ellen_wildman or on ellenwildman.com.

1

Already Whole

So God created human beings in his own image. In the image
of God he created them; male and female he created them.

GENESIS 1:27

Does it seem like everyone around you is getting "work done"?
Seemingly out of nowhere, Botox, plastic surgery, fillers, and
more have become the norm. A friend got her forehead wrinkles
removed, your neighbor got lip filler, and a gal at church is plan-
ning a tummy tuck. While there is nothing inherently wrong with
this, it can make those of us who don't want or can't afford to do
these procedures feel like we are missing out on something. But
even before medspas, plastic surgery, or doctors' offices, before
we tried to find our worth in fixing ourselves, we were created in
God's image.

Imago Dei is a Latin phrase meaning "image of God." As described
in today's Scripture, humanity is the imago Dei, created "in his own
image" (Genesis 1:27). You reflect God in
your very being as who you are right now.
While we can look at our body and see flaws
that need to be remedied, God looks at us
and sees Himself reflected. Just as an artist
meticulously paints a portrait of someone dear
to them, reflecting that person's appearance

**God looks at us
and sees Himself
reflected.**

in their painting while also incorporating their personality through
use of brushstroke and color, you were crafted by God as an image

pointing back to Him. Your imago Dei status cannot be removed or destroyed—it's who you are, made in the image of God.

What freedom there is in knowing that you are made in God's image! Just as that artist bursts with pride over their finished portrait, imagine how much more God cares for you as one created to reflect His goodness and His love. If you've faced mental or physical illness, abuse, heartbreak, or another difficult situation, no matter how much you feel your life has been marred by trial, you still have the status of God's image bearer. Nothing you can face or do will take away this truth or make you less worthy of God's love and pride. You are created in His image, and that's a fact.[1] No work necessary.

EMBRACING WHOLENESS

I am already whole, loved, and worthy of love. I was created in the image of a holy, loving, and creative God.

2

Fearfully and Wonderfully Made

I praise you because I am fearfully and wonderfully made;
your works are wonderful; I know that full well.

PSALM 139:14 NIV

What difference does it make in your day-to-day life to know that you are created in the image of God? How does this affect you as you tackle that overwhelming pile of dishes, study for that intimidating test, or deal with some unexpected car trouble that sucks your savings account dry? How does this knowledge meet you in the underwhelmingly ordinary moments?

Our Scripture today explains that not only are you crafted in God's image, God created you "fearfully and wonderfully" (Psalm 139:14 NIV). Fear here doesn't mean God was afraid when He crafted you, or that He designed you to be afraid, but instead points to the holy process of your creation—one that deserves our reverence and awe. The word *fear* in the original Hebrew language would be better translated "awe" or "reverence." It demonstrates a sacred process, one filled with intention and care. And in moments where you feel lost, frustrated, or overwhelmed, it is immensely comforting to know that the Lord took care to create you just as you are and loves you for how you show up today. Stressors will come and go, but your status as one beloved by God will remain the same forever.

Whether your day feels ordinary or is filled with anxiety, whether you feel confident in your skin as you navigate the world or face negative self-talk and heightened stress around others, you can always come back to the truth that when God created you, it was not by chance. You are a work of His hands, and therefore you are wonderful. You can walk through each day with the confidence of one created and treasured by the King of the universe. And, just maybe, this knowledge will help you walk a little lighter as you face the day. Knowing and accepting that you are made in the image of God will propel you through each moment with the relief and comfort of one who is treasured simply because you exist.

EMBRACING WHOLENESS

As one who is fearfully and wonderfully made, I can face each day and show up as I am. God is always with me.

3

An Imago Dei Worldview

See how very much our Father loves us, for he
calls us his children, and that is what we are!

1 JOHN 3:1

Theologian Francis A. Schaeffer wrote in his book *Escape from Reason*: "People today are trying to hang on to the dignity of man, and they do not know how to, because they have lost the truth that man is made in the image of God."[2] As we grasp more deeply what it means to be created in the image of God, we ought also to consider the community-wide impact of this message. For it was not simply you alone who was crafted with love and care in His image, but all of those around you.

As today's verse explains, the God who created us imago Dei calls us all His children when we put our trust in Him: those we get along with easily and those who wear us down; those we admire and those we avoid; those we adore with our whole heart and those we find hard to love. Yes, we are all created in His image and accepted by His unending love when we receive His gift of salvation, flaws and all. So as you go through your day balancing grocery shopping, soccer games, Zoom meetings, and doctor's appointments, encountering any number of people, how would viewing each person you meet through the lens of their image-bearer nature change you?

Seeing others through an imago Dei worldview reminds us of the inherent dignity and value of every human being. Regardless of someone else's background, ethnicity, body size, social status, or economic situation, they will always be worthy of respect (see also Galatians 3:28). And if they are a fellow believer, God calls them His son or daughter, loved intimately just like you. Even if you are having a bad day or are frustrated with a bureaucratic process, with waiting in line, or with one of life's many inconveniences, perhaps reminding yourself of another's inherent worth will help you to take a minute prior to reacting in a way you may regret. There is unity to be found in the community of imago Dei, and this awareness can promote empathy and compassion in our hurried hearts as we encounter others.

EMBRACING WHOLENESS

Just as I am created in the image of a loving God, so are those I encounter every day. Therefore, I can ask the Lord to increase my empathy and compassion for others.

Christian Self-Love

We love because he first loved us.

1 JOHN 4:19 NIV

You've likely heard the term *self-love* at some point in the last few years. Cultural self-love tells you that

- you are perfect just as you are;
- you can boost your confidence by comparing yourself to those around you that you perceive as failing;
- and that you should love yourself without ever changing.

But this narrative goes against what the Bible says. The truth is that

- you are made whole in Christ (1 Thessalonians 5:23);
- you can only truly be fulfilled when you seek the approval of God, not of people (Galatians 1:10);
- and you will sin and fail, but you are redeemed by the grace of the Lord (Romans 3:23–24).

The foundation of self-love from a Christian perspective lies in the truth that we are created in the image of God, and we are defined by His unending love and grace toward us. Christian self-love roots itself in God's love for you, His creation. His love is so great that when you love yourself, you delight God—He sees that you get a glimpse of how He feels about you. God loves you so much, and He is honored when you love yourself, even as you grow and change throughout your life (see 1 John 4:19, 1 Timothy 4:12).

There may be things about yourself that you find hard to love, and that's okay. He understands. It's an act of care to look at yourself and acknowledge that you are far from perfect, but that none of your faults or failures separate you from God and His love for you. Embracing self-love in this way means extending the same love and grace to yourself that the Lord extends to you.

We can acknowledge that we are imperfect while knowing that we are loved by a perfect God. Self-love is not self-centeredness—putting your desires above others and thinking of yourself as better than everyone else (see Romans 12:3). Self-love is believing the truths of what God says about you and applying these truths to your life. It is possible to appreciate who you are even while fostering physical, spiritual, or mental growth. Christian self-love is not only possible; it presents the opportunity to connect more deeply to your Creator.

EMBRACING WHOLENESS

I accept who I am right now without judgment. I am immeasurably loved by God.

Anti-Diet Revolution

"Everything is permissible for me," but not everything
is beneficial. "Everything is permissible for me,"
but I will not be mastered by anything.

1 CORINTHIANS 6:12 CSB

Fifty-six percent of women have tried to lose weight in the last year.[3] And while the pursuit of weight loss isn't inherently bad, for most of us, the pursuit of a smaller body is loaded with additional shame, self-hatred, and struggle. Dieting is often synonymous with restriction and limitation. But God did not create you to hate yourself into a smaller frame. You are made in God's image. This means that He knew the exact body shape you would have, and He blessed it. The truth is, it is better to be in a larger body as you pursue wholeness in Christ than to shame and contain yourself into a more societally acceptable size.

Today's verse describes that "'everything is permissible for me,' but not everything is beneficial" (1 Corinthians 6:12 CSB). Sure, you can diet if you truly feel this is the best course of action for you. But it is rare for the pursuit of a smaller body to be a baggage-free endeavor. According to the *Journal of the Academy of Nutrition and Dietetics*, "Starvation and self-imposed dieting appear to result in eating binges once food is available and in psychological manifestations such as preoccupation with food and eating, increased emotional responsiveness and dysphoria, and distractibility."[4] Not only is dieting not beneficial, it can also easily become an obsession, impacting your mental and physical health.

What would it look like to trust God with your body? To bring your fears, your insecurities, and your feelings to Him, trusting that He created you as you are for a purpose? As the imago Dei, you can be free from the chains and the shame of diet culture. You can refuse to put yourself on an unnecessary diet, because you know that developing a positive relationship with your body is more about your mental health and your view of yourself than your physical body anyway. You can start your own revolution, refusing to be mastered by the lies of your insecurity and instead speak the truth of your beloved-ness over your life.

EMBRACING WHOLENESS

Losing weight and dieting will not soothe my pain or suddenly make me happier. Rooting my life in my relationship with God is the only thing that can set me free and bring me lasting peace.

6

Celebrating Your Body's Abilities

The LORD is my strength and my shield; my heart
trusts in him, and he helps me. My heart leaps
for joy, and with my song I praise him.

PSALM 28:7 NIV

We can describe strength in many ways. *Merriam-Webster* alone lists eight different definitions, including the "capacity for exertion or endurance," the "power to resist force," and "solidity" or "toughness."[5] Even this one source proves that strength comes in all forms and fashions, looking different for each of us. You might have a physical disability, trauma, mental health issues, or past hurt that sometimes prohibit you from seeing yourself as a strong person. Take heart, for strength is a beautifully multidimensional thing. When we broaden our own definition of strength, we see how strong we all really are.

No matter where you find yourself, there is space to celebrate your body's abilities and your strength. Perhaps it just takes embracing a broader understanding of the word *strength* to discover what was within you all along! Did you answer an email or text today, demonstrating your brain's abilities to communicate with your body in an informed and timely way? Perhaps you went on a walk or jogged with a friend, a reminder of your legs' ability to act without even thinking about it. Or maybe you had a hard conversation with a family member, demonstrating your deep ability to show empathy and compassion for others you care about. No matter what strength looks like in your body, it is there. From your brain to your hands to your belly to your feet! You don't have to be physically strong like her or mentally tough like him—you can be strong like you.

The Lord Himself reminds us that strength can be defined in different ways. Isaiah 40:28 describes God's physical strength, that He never grows tired or weary. Ephesians 6:10 explains that He is mighty. Matthew 19:26 says God is omnipotent, meaning He is all-powerful. When you first see yourself as one created in the image of this strong and powerful God, and then allow this knowledge to seep into your bones, you may just find yourself with an increased ability to see your body for what it is: strong.

EMBRACING WHOLENESS

I celebrate the unique abilities of my body today. May the strength I have within move me to praise God for who I am.

7

Naked and Unashamed

Now the man and his wife were both
naked, but they felt no shame.
GENESIS 2:25

Adam and Eve stood before God and before each other naked
and unashamed ... phew. Can you imagine? In the garden
of Eden, the perfect world not yet marred by sin, human beings
could be completely transparent and authentic. Not only were
they physically naked, but they were also emotionally, spiritually,
and relationally naked. They held nothing back from one another,
and most importantly, they hid nothing from God. They were free
from shame because they had nothing to hide. We can learn from
their example.

Today's verse concludes the creation account, the seven days
during which God fashioned the entire world, culminating in His
creation of humankind in His own image (Genesis 1:27). While
this alone is worthy of profound praise, today's Scripture (Genesis 2:25) further enriches our understanding of this narrative by
revealing that, in the idyllic garden of Eden, Adam and Eve lived
unashamedly, fully embracing their physical bodies as part of God's
magnificent creation. This is important because it tells us that body
shame was never God's intention. It only occurred when sin later
entered the world. In Genesis 3, after Adam and Eve ate from the
Tree of Knowledge of Good and Evil and, as a result, sin entered
the world, they suddenly realized their nakedness and immediately

covered themselves. They scrambled to hide from God's presence. Sin brought body shame and guilt and separation from our Creator. And yet, we can return to Him. We may feel shame, embarrassment, or even hatred toward our body. But just as God graciously provided clothing to Adam and Eve when they realized they were naked, He meets us in our mess with love, understanding, and grace.

Adam and Eve covered themselves because they felt physically exposed. As a result of the brokenness the fall created, we cover ourselves too, in all sorts of ways. This world is now marked by body shame, an understanding that everyone has something they don't like about themselves. And while culture would tell us to use these negative beliefs as motivation to punish ourselves into smaller bodies, better habits, or tighter clothes, God tells a different story. God asks us to bring our shame to Him, giving it over to Him and exchanging it for authenticity. While we cannot return to the perfection of the garden of Eden, we can create space for God's grace to work through our brokenness, bringing healing and restoration. We can each work on loving our body as an act of praising God, being transparent with Him and unashamed.

EMBRACING WHOLENESS

I can release body shame freely, knowing it is something God never intended me to carry.

8

Partnering with Your Body

What is mankind that you are mindful of them,
human beings that you care for them?

PSALM 8:4 NIV

Many of us have spent our lives working against our bodies. You may see your own body as the enemy, working against your progress and your productivity. Because, let's be honest, having a body is really inconvenient. It cries out for food and rest when we just want to keep going, keep working, keep checking things off the to-do list. Getting sick or hurt never happens at a convenient time; it's never an experience we enjoy. Our bodies ask for care, and we answer with a solid no when we turn around and prioritize other things over listening to our own needs, even good things like social events, friends, and hobbies. But a big part of learning to accept and even love our bodies is to cease working against them, ignoring their needs and wants, and instead to partner with our bodies to build a relationship of trust and understanding.

We often feel like we simply own our bodies, and many of us are begrudging owners. They're something we have, something we're tied to. We even ignore our bodies' needs at times, because these bodies are just our property; they're at our disposal. When we see our bodies simply as something we own, we can more easily rationalize the lies diet culture spews—lies that tell us that we can only love our bodies if we subject them to a new trend, diet, or needle. However, when we decide to partner with our bodies, tuning in to their signals and learning to build trust with those signals we find that we can trust our bodily intuition as we make our physical bodies our homes. Pain, hunger, sadness, joy—they all tell us something is going on. And when we partner with our bodies, we ask ourselves, *How can I help?*

Partnering with your body is a more complex step in the journey to healing your self-image. What it really comes down to is simply asking your body what it needs and listening to it when it's trying to tell you something. As we learn to trust our own bodies, we will also learn to trust our Creator in deeper ways, knowing that He cares for us.

EMBRACING WHOLENESS

I choose today to partner with my body, building trust, care, and connection with it.

Your Body Will Change

There is a time for everything, and a season
for every activity under the heavens.
ECCLESIASTES 3:1 NIV

We've all done it—used pictures of our past selves as ammo to fuel our body embarrassment and even self-hatred. It doesn't matter if it was one year, five years, or more than ten years ago—we subject our current bodies to comparison that is harsh and only ever judgmental. Whether your thought process sounds something like—*Wow, I was so thin then. I've really lost control,* or something like *I can't believe how heavy I was in that picture; I'm so glad I'm good now*—the blame and the body shame remain the same. We cannot fully experience body respect and begin to move toward body love until we accept that our bodies change.

Throughout your adult life, your body will undergo many changes. Sure, you're no longer in the milestone months of infancy or the growth spurts of middle school and high school, but your body is still forever transforming. You may gain weight; you may lose weight. You may develop a medical condition that affects your limbs or find yourself needing glasses, hearing aids, or other help as your body ages. Even illness, which God did not intend for our bodies from the beginning, can't take away your inherent worth. No change that your body undergoes will ever make your body bad or wrong. If we cannot accept that our body will change throughout our lives, we will forever be trapped in a mentality that our body is not good. The truth is that your body is good because it is part of what it means to be created in the image of God. And any changes you encounter do not mar or diminish or prohibit that goodness.

When we reflect on how our body may have looked different in the past, we have the opportunity to practice gentle self-compassion. Sure, your body was different then, but perhaps you now have a better self-image, have worked on your relationship with food, or have a better connection with your family. Our body changes don't tell the full story, so we offer compassion to our former selves that were likely doing the best they could. Now is our opportunity to redeem our relationship with our body forever, ever affirming that—no matter how much our body changes throughout our lifetime—it will always be good.

EMBRACING WHOLENESS

My body will change throughout my life, and that is okay. God created me, and He said my body is good.

Your body is good because it is part of what it means to be created in the image of God.

Both/And

Therefore, there is now no condemnation
for those in Christ Jesus.
ROMANS 8:1 CSB

There's a misconception with body positivity that to accept yourself also means to permanently halt any growth or change you desire for your body—but this just isn't true. Instead, it is a both/and. You can both respect, trust, and love your body as it is right now and also desire to grow, change, and even alter it. It *doesn't* mean you're bad at self-love if you want your body to feel different, to know you want to sleep more instead of staying up late scrolling on your phone. It *doesn't* mean you lack respect for your body now if you start to prioritize movement, strengthening your muscles. It *doesn't* mean you can't accept your current body if you make diet changes, adding in more fruits and vegetables because you've noticed doing this makes you feel more energized throughout the day. It *does* mean that—as you navigate the tricky gray area of the both/and—noticing and rejecting shame and blame are pivotal to your healing and growth.

The hardest part of this both/and process—accepting your current body while noticing areas you'd like to change—is that this dichotomy is often steeped in shame and blame. Sometimes these feelings are even used as motivators for healthy living. But shame and blame ultimately distance you from the goodness of body acceptance, body respect, and body love; they use your own self-hatred as fuel. But the fuel of self-disgust will always burn out and leave you worse off than you were before. On the contrary, when you are fueled by body respect, you are propelled by the desire to learn more about treating your body well. This curiosity, this self-awareness, will continue to stoke the flames of respect for your body. The match that sets it all ablaze is the truth of your beloved-ness as God's creation.

As today's verse highlights, God does not condemn, shame, or guilt us into spiritual transformation. By extension, it's not part of His character to guilt us into physical transformation either. So why should we do this to ourselves? Today, you can acknowledge and appreciate your body's uniqueness and strengths while knowing there are things you'd like to change. Remember that wanting change is natural, but we can adjust these desires to be driven by self-love and self-improvement rather than self-criticism, fostering an environment where any changes are deliberate and kind while maintaining a foundation of self-love.

EMBRACING WHOLENESS

I accept my body as it is, even as I acknowledge there are ways I'd like to change.

Dominion

Then God said, "Let us make human beings in our image, to
be like us. They will reign over the fish in the sea, the birds
in the sky, the livestock, all the wild animals on the earth,
and the small animals that scurry along the ground."

GENESIS 1:26

Genesis 1:26 is the core text for a working framework of humanity as the imago Dei (image of God). This text doesn't just tell us of our treasured place as His image bearers; it also explains that humankind is to "reign" over the rest of God's creation. Some translations interpret this as "rule over" (NIV) or "have dominion over" (ESV). Regardless of exactly how the original Hebrew is translated, this passage means that God has called us to exercise His authority over His creation! Psalm 8:6 echoes this: "You gave them charge of everything you made, putting all things under their authority."

Because both our creation in God's image and our work done in that image are proclaimed in this verse, we can surmise that we represent His image faithfully when we exercise rule and reign over creation. But what does this mean for us today? In ancient times, life involved a lot more interaction with other created beings—through fishing, farming, and tending the earth for food; battling predators for survival; or caring for the earth to nourish oneself, one's family, and one's animals. But unless you have a homestead in the Alaskan wilderness, you likely aren't fending off wild beasts, picking a chicken out of the coop for dinner, or harvesting in the field alongside your ox. Instead, we fulfill His holy calling today when we seek to display God in our daily work at our desk or in meetings, when we care for those placed in our circle of influence, and when we try to take care of the earth to the best of our ability for the next generation.

Our dominion over God's creation comes as a reflection of the image of God within us. It looks like stewarding what we have, caring for others, and reflecting that image to those around us. It means leaning into your gifts, your skills, and the unique ways you reflect the image of God to serve His people and better the world. We can praise God today for the incredible gift of His image at work within us.

EMBRACING WHOLENESS

I am created in God's image and charged by Him to rule over the earth. I can do this today by stewarding my resources and my relationships well.

Speak Life

Don't use foul or abusive language. Let everything
you say be good and helpful, so that your words will
be an encouragement to those who hear them.

EPHESIANS 4:29

Life is full of inconveniences. You forget your password and have to spend ten minutes setting a new one. Your phone dies right when you are about to head out on a trip where you need GPS. You leave five minutes late for dinner with a friend and get stuck at the train tracks, waiting for a slow train to pass. So many things can go wrong in this life, things we have no control over, like technology, transportation, and other people. When the inconveniences pile up, it's tempting to react with annoyance, frustration, or harshness. The fact that the average American spends more than seven months of their lifetime waiting in line is enough to make even the most patient of us feel a little on edge.[6]

We can all recall a time when someone around us responded totally inappropriately to a stranger—maybe on a plane, at the DMV, or in line at a coffee shop. We learn from these awkward and disheartening interactions that when we face life's unavoidable frustrations, and we will, what matters most is our reaction. Sometimes we react in a regrettable way not because someone caused the problem we are stewing over, but they are just unknowingly in our path while we brew in our impatience. In these moments, it feels easy to act with harshness or to say something we regret. But we have the opportunity to speak life. Proverbs 18:21 says: "The tongue can bring death or life."

Being a person who speaks life starts with the Holy Spirit. As we wade through the inconveniences of life, we can seek the peace of the Holy Spirit that calms us and helps make us more aware of those around us. 1 Peter 3:11 says we are to "search for peace, and work to maintain it." A simple prayer for a calm spirit in the midst of a crazymaking situation can make all the difference. Along with this, we speak life by affirming and encouraging those we interact with, knowing they may be discouraged by others' words of death. A kind word to the drive-through employee, the customer-service desk attendant, or the IT helpline can shift the trajectory of someone's day in immeasurable ways.

Luke 6:45 says it well: "What you say flows from what is in your heart."

EMBRACING WHOLENESS

My words have the potential to shape hearts and minds, making each interaction an opportunity to spread joy and kindness. May the Holy Spirit help me speak life today.

The Promise of a Heavenly Body

Our citizenship is in heaven, and we eagerly wait for a Savior
from there, the Lord Jesus Christ. He will transform the body
of our humble condition into the likeness of his glorious body,
by the power that enables him to subject everything to himself.

PHILIPPIANS 3:20–21 CSB

While we are here on earth, we will often find ourselves pre-occupied with our physical body—our appearance, our health, and our comfort. We strive to maintain our body, nourishing and caring for it as we embark on a journey to heal our relationship with it. And in the midst of all of this, Scripture reminds us of a more profound truth: our ultimate citizenship is in heaven, and a new, greater heavenly body awaits those of us who trust in Jesus. As Paul writes in 2 Corinthians 5, "For we know that if our earthly tent we live in is destroyed, we have a building from God, an eternal dwelling in the heavens, not made with hands" (v. 1 CSB).

We do not know what our heavenly body will look like; this mystery will only be revealed in eternity. Revelation 21:4 (CSB) does tell us, however, that in heaven, "He will wipe away every tear from their eyes. Death will be no more; grief, crying, and pain will be no more, because the previous things have passed away." So, while our body here on earth may carry illness, disease, or trauma, this will all be forgotten when we are in heaven with the Lord! This promise of transformation into a heavenly body can remind us that our struggles in this world are temporary, and for those of us who trust in God, our eternity will be one in a new, better body. Our heavenly body will be free from the limitations and imperfections that we experience today.

One day we will be clothed in glory, radiant in the presence of God, and equipped with a new body, overjoyed to spend eternity with Him. In the meantime, we hold on to the hope of this promise even as we grapple with our earthly body. Today, allow yourself to picture a body with no limitations, no sickness, no trauma, no self-consciousness. That promise of total and complete body freedom is a reality, an eternal promise, when you put your trust in Jesus.

EMBRACING WHOLENESS

As I process through my relationship with my body here on earth, I am reminded that my true home is in heaven. My heavenly body is a hope that sustains me today.

Embracing Body Diversity

From one man he has made every nationality to live over the whole earth and has determined their appointed times and the boundaries of where they live. He did this so that they might seek God, and perhaps they might reach out and find him, though he is not far from each one of us.

ACTS 17:26–27 CSB

Every human being on the planet has come from Adam, the image of God created in Genesis (see Genesis 2:7), as referenced in today's passage. Because we are descendants of this first man, God could have created us all to look and act the same, but He chose not to. Body diversity—the difference from person to person in body size, shape, skin color, abilities—is not by accident. Without incorporating body diversity acceptance into our own lives, beauty standards become narrow ideals, causing almost all of us to miss the mark. When we believe one type of body is the "right" type, we intrinsically accept that our body is wrong when it doesn't measure up to these impossible and ever-changing standards. We begin to think that *we* are wrong: physically, mentally, or emotionally. But when we decide instead to claim the beauty found in body diversity,

God created you in His image, and He created your neighbors, friends, family, coworkers, and barista in that image too.

we can celebrate both our own unique body and the distinct, striking beauty in men and women around us.

We see the goodness of body diversity when we start with a mindset grounded in the goodness of all creation. God created you in His image, and He created your neighbors, friends, family, coworkers, and barista in that image too. He said His creation was "good" (Genesis 1:31). Your body is good. Their body is good. Body diversity celebrates this multifaceted goodness! Take a moment and acknowledge what is unique about your body. Instead of judging your differences, try seeing them through the eyes of God and honoring Him for making you different from others.

We affirm that God knew what He was doing in creating humankind when we rejoice in our differences instead of striving to achieve a homogeneity that God never required of us. So, body diversity first begins with body acceptance. This will not be an overnight transformation. But when we invest in our relationship with our Creator while endeavoring to speak kindly about our own body, we will naturally notice a shift in our perspective. When we follow diverse social media accounts, compliment others with non-appearance–based remarks, and strive to heal our own view of our body, we will begin to celebrate the diversity of God's creation . . . just as He intended.

EMBRACING WHOLENESS

Body diversity is good. My body is good.

Scars, Marks, and Acne

You are absolutely beautiful, my darling;
there is no imperfection in you.
SONG OF SOLOMON 4:7 CSB

Our body carries physical signs of our story, of our complicated and stunning life. We have scars—signs of trauma, of accidents, of experiences we might wish to forget. We have marks—moles, freckles, birthmarks. We have acne, or had acne—signs of hormone changes, puberty, or stress. These scars, marks, and acne make up a part of who we are. They are on our body, and therefore a part of us. Signs of growth, change, and survival. They remind us that we are alive. They tell the story that our body is good.

It may seem implausible to you that you can see scars, marks, and acne in a positive light. Perhaps your scars carry reminders of suffering, your freckles make you feel self-conscious, or your acne feels painful or burdensome. Drawing attention to these physical signs distinguishing your body from others can be uncomfortable. At the same time, the uniqueness of your body is beautiful. These marks tell your story. Your body explains what you've been through, a story of healing and transformation. These marks do not define you, but they oftentimes demand to be noticed. When you only look upon everything with disgust—the map of moles covering your arms, the surgery scar on your knee, or the acne along your chin—you devalue your body for the way it's carried you through life. What if instead, we see our body's distinctive qualities as a reflection of the truth that God is an intentional Creator and continues to call us *good*?

No matter what scars, blemishes, bumps, and bruises your body holds, it is good. Ephesians 2:10 says that you are "God's masterpiece," and a masterpiece isn't made by mistake. Take a moment today to reflect on the bumps, marks, and moles that make you, you. Even if you initially feel shame, discomfort, or self-consciousness, know that God is with you in these feelings. He will walk alongside you on your journey to body acceptance as you are reminded over and over again that your body tells a story of redemption, of progress, and of goodness.[7]

EMBRACING WHOLENESS

My body tells a unique story, and this story is good. With God's help, I can find acceptance and even love for my bumps, scars, and marks.

16

Pleasing God, Not People

Am I now trying to win the approval of human beings, or of God? Or am I trying to please people? If I were still trying to please people, I would not be a servant of Christ.

GALATIANS 1:10 NIV

We all long for approval. When you get an unexpected compliment from a stranger, your heart fills with joy and a sense of validation. When your yearly review goes surprisingly well, you're filled with relief and excitement. When a friend reminds you of how dear you are to them, you feel yourself relax and maybe even release a breath you didn't know you were holding in. And while none of these experiences and feelings are inherently bad, when we begin to look only to others to remind us of our value and worth, we can become obsessed with pleasing them to garner compliments and praise. But how do we look to God instead for approval, knowing that the words of others feel more concrete and easier to understand at times?

The journey of releasing our need for the approval of others begins with acknowledgment. When you realize how much stock you are placing in others' opinions, you may feel a holy unsettlement. This is the Spirit of God reminding you that you were not created to live motivated by the praise of other human beings. No! You are created in the image of God, and God longs for you to live for Him. This is not to say that He will be disappointed in you if your heart thrills at a compliment or your day is made when you get positive feedback. It's more about intention. Do you feel yourself becoming obsessed with collecting compliments, or can you rest in the truth of who God says you are?

While God's approval is not spoken in human words, it's actually more concrete than we think, laid out clearly in the pages of Scripture. The truth is that, in Christ, you are redeemed, your life has a unique purpose, you are created for good works, you are free. God says you are chosen, you are loved, you are treasured. When you trust God with your life and enter into a relationship with Him, your motivations shift.

Three things are true:

(1) You already have the approval of God because you were created by Him; (2) He loves you beyond your wildest understanding; and (3) when you go throughout your day responding to and rooted in His love, God is proud of you. He "approves" of your actions because they are motivated by a heart that seeks after Him.

EMBRACING WHOLENESS

I was not created to live for the approval of others. God accepts and loves me just as I am, and He says I am treasured.

Temple Care

Don't you realize that your body is the temple of the Holy
Spirit, who lives in you and was given to you by God?
You do not belong to yourself, for God bought you with
a high price. So you must honor God with your body.

1 CORINTHIANS 6:19–20

Most of us treat places of worship, like churches, with a certain respect because they are the settings in which we meet with God. We should treat our bodies in the same way. Because followers of Jesus always have the Holy Spirit with them. He dwells within our very bodies, making the place of worship our physical bodies themselves.[8] He is the Comforter, Teacher, Leader, guiding and growing our relationship with Christ.

So, how do we care for our bodies with the same reverence we show to our church buildings?

Maybe you've heard 1 Corinthians 6:19–20 before in relation to exercising, dieting, or even restricting. Maybe this passage was plastered on your gym's wall, or your mom recited it as she gave you no-carb bread, which tasted eerily like cardboard. While it's true that these verses speak to taking care of yourself, they are not advocating for an obsession with extreme fitness, dangerous dieting, and punishing your body to fit it into a certain jean size or socially acceptable body type. To "honor God with your body" is to show yourself respect, care, and appreciation.

But where do we start? What if you listened to your body's needs more closely, finding out what foods and levels of physical activity make you feel best? This could include joyful movement like dancing in the kitchen while making dinner, taking walks with friends, or tapping into your inner child and buying a scooter. Building awareness around your mental health is also important, perhaps going to therapy, asking for help when you need it, and forming close relationships where you can be honest and feel safe. And let's not forget the importance of emotional health, feeling and processing through your feelings as you are able. These are all aspects of your body, ways in which you can become more aware of and at peace with the temple you spend every day in. Appreciating your body's limits, learning to rest when you need it and getting active when you feel it is right shows your body that you care for it. Taking care of your temple is hard work, but it's work that pleases God and benefits you.

EMBRACING WHOLENESS

Taking care of my body—physically, emotionally, and mentally—honors God and makes me more at home in the body God gave me.

18

Eve, Our Mother

The man named his wife Eve because she
was the mother of all the living.

GENESIS 3:20 CSB

Do you think Eve had a belly button? Because she was created by God fully formed, no umbilical cord attached her to her mother at birth. In fact, she came from a man (created from Adam's rib). Kind of crazy to think about! Really, Eve pioneered many roles: she was the first woman, the first mother, the first to fall into sin. And while we often emphasize the sin part of her story, we can discover goodness in Eve, too.

Eve began her life with a closeness to God we can only imagine. She was placed in an idyllic setting, the garden of Eden, and knew only a trusting, loving relationship with her Creator. We don't know how Eve felt about her body, but we can assume that—because she knew she was created in God's image, and because no outside pressures like diet culture or societal standards existed at the time—she embraced her physicality. Genesis 1:28 (CSB) tells us that upon her creation alongside Adam, she was blessed by God and directed to "be fruitful, multiply, fill the earth, and subdue it. Rule the fish of the sea, the birds of the sky, and every creature that crawls on the earth." So, Eve is our mother. Her name even sounds like the Hebrew word for *life-giver*. And Eve is our example of a leader. While we aren't given the specifics of Adam and Eve's relationship, we see in Eve a confidence to work and lead alongside her husband.

Following Adam and Eve's sin and subsequent expulsion from the garden, they remained obedient to God's directive to "be fruitful" and "multiply" (v. 28 csb). While they had other children, of the children Eve gave birth to, three are named: Cain, Abel, and Seth.

Eve was far from perfect, and yet she is a pillar of our faith, an example of blessing and then of redemption and forgiveness. We remember Eve as our mother in faith, the woman who faced challenges and temptations but ultimately found redemption and purpose in God's plan. Through her story, we are reminded that God's love, grace, and forgiveness are available to us all.

EMBRACING WHOLENESS

I look to Eve—who lived out her calling to reflect the image of her Creator—as I boldly embrace who I am created to be today.

Weighing In

Yet I will certainly bring health and healing to it and will indeed
heal them. I will let them experience the abundance of true peace.

JEREMIAH 33:6 CSB

Certain comments stick with us for a lifetime. Rude, hurtful,
and cutting remarks that replay in our mind even years later,
especially when they hit at a recurring insecurity or pain point. And,
for many of us, those comments are centered around our weight.
As you work toward a healed relationship with your body, may
this truth undergird your experience: your weight alone does not
indicate your level of health.

If someone has made the correlation between your weight and
your health—telling you that you were too small or too large or
calling you foul names—please know that was wrong of them. Bully-
ing is never okay. The truth is, people of every size experience high
cholesterol, high blood pressure, illness, and disease. People of every
size face mental health crisis and emotional and relational turmoil.
Research supports this: Researchers at UCLA and the University of
Minnesota have concluded that you cannot tell a person is healthy
based exclusively on their weight.[9] People of all body sizes can be fit,
healthy, and happy. As Linda Bacon writes: "The only way to solve
the weight problem is to stop making weight a problem—to stop
judging ourselves and others by our size. Weight is not an effective
measure of attractiveness, moral character, or health."[10]

This is your opportunity to reject the lie someone may have

spoken over you about your body. With God's help, you can refuse the widely held belief that thin = healthy. You can deny cultural messaging that reinforces this lie by focusing more on your holistic health—mind, body, soul. God didn't create a skinnier or fitter or more beautiful version of you waiting to be unleashed when you just get it together. No, God created you in His image in the here and now. Our body diversity is intentional, and it is beautiful. Even if you don't love your body just yet, may you bravely reject the idea today that your weight is the only marker of health.

EMBRACING WHOLENESS

I reject the lie that thin = healthy. May God help me to let go of the pursuit of unrealistic goals and impossible body standards and instead embrace what true health and wholeness look like for me.

20

The Beauty of Finitude

God is not human, that he should lie, not a human
being, that he should change his mind. Does he speak
and then not act? Does he promise and not fulfill?

NUMBERS 23:19 NIV

D o you ever feel an inner but indescribable pull that tells you
to push, to finish things as quickly as possible, to do as much
as you can in as little time as you can? It's a hurried pace that our
heart, mind, and body unconsciously agree to, matching the pace
of our culture that preaches that more is better. Hustle equates
accomplishment, and accepting our humanness is acceptance of
failure. But God preaches a different and better message, one that
has the power to realign our pace. It says: God created us as finite
on purpose. You were never meant to do it all.

God does not grow tired, nor does He get stuck in the toil and
grind of daily tasks like we do (see Isaiah 40). Because God created us in His image, He could have bestowed this same strength
upon us, but He choose not to. Therefore, God had purpose in
creating us as beings that need rest and reflection. Beings that
need time, thought, and space to heal. And this recognition and
acceptance of our finitude is an opportunity for praise, for us to
get off the hamster wheel of production and accept that we can't
do it all, and that we'll never be able to. There is freedom and rest
in the acceptance of our humanness.

To slow down this rush we feel inside, we must look to God as our guide instead of looking to the world around us. The world around us will make us feel that we are only falling behind, that we are not doing enough, that we don't have time to do it all. But with God as our guide, we remember that we aren't meant to do it all, and we can release the pressure to. We can take our time with what is important, knowing that God is in control of our days, our hours, our minutes. When we come to Him in prayer, asking Him to calm our spirit and help us realign our priorities, we can take comfort in our finiteness, knowing that we were created this way on purpose. Our humanness is not a defect or an accident, but a reminder that we have limited energy and time, and with God, we can steward it well.

EMBRACING WHOLENESS

Today, I embrace that God created me with limits on purpose. I look to Him to calm my hurried spirit within, knowing that He will guide me through each day.

21

Your Body Is Your Home

For we know that if the earthly tent we live in is
destroyed, we have a building from God, an eternal
house in heaven, not built by human hands.

2 CORINTHIANS 5:1 NIV

Your body is more than a vessel. Yes, it is a divine creation, inhabited by your soul, serving as the dwelling place for the Holy Spirit. But while you are here on earth, your body is also your home. You will spend every minute, every day, every year, in that same physical body. It will carry you through different illnesses, all manner of emotions, and untold celebrations. It will see you through travel, sustain you in exhaustion, and ask you to rest when you are just plain worn out. And, if you have a relationship with Christ, one day it will be exchanged for a heavenly body. But until then, it is your home . . . so it's time to get cozy.

Many of us find disconnecting with our physical body easier than doing the work of making our bodily home a loving, safe, special place to be. Like someone who has moved across the country one too many times, we think it's easier to never really put down roots, not to get too comfortable. The fear of facing deep insecurities, the ease of looking at the negatives, or the natural response to give in to the cultural narratives about our body seem simpler than sinking into and embracing the truth. While avoiding the truth may be easier, if we are to truly heal the relationship with our body, we must fully accept our bodily home. For we are given one body, and if we do not treat it as our home, we can never really experience all that this one full and beautiful life has for us. If we live our life disassociating from our body, caring only for our soul, we miss the opportunity for a deeper peace and a greater joy that comes with living as an embodied person.

A healthy connection with our bodily home starts with acknowledging our Creator's good work, knowing that our status as His image bearer gives innate worth to our earthly body. And when we see our home as one of great worth, we can start to build body trust. We cannot feel safe and loved without this trust, which acknowledges that our body will carry us through whatever we face. As we journey toward body trust, body respect, and body love, we set a foundation that says our body is our home, so we deserve to feel safe, loved, and held there.

EMBRACING WHOLENESS

My body is my home. I am worthy of self-discovery, and with God's help, I can learn to feel more at home here.

If we are to
truly heal the
relationship with
our body, we must
fully accept our
bodily home.

22

All Creation Praises

Praise the LORD. Praise the LORD from the heavens; praise
him in the heights above. Praise him, all his angels; praise him,
all his heavenly hosts. Praise him, sun and moon; praise him,
all you shining stars. Praise him, you highest heavens and you
waters above the skies. Let them praise the name of the LORD,
for at his command they were created.

PSALM 148:1–5 NIV

In Genesis 1, God spoke the world into existence. He formed and
fashioned everything—from puffy clouds to the untamed sea,
from blossoming fruit trees to barren deserts, from daring hawks
to tiny centipedes. Today's passage recalls this creation narrative,
showing all the earth worshiping God, based not on what He did
in the past, or on what we hope He will do in the future, but on His
identity as the magnificent Creator. Each element of His creation
worships Him for who He is. Some commentators even suggest that
creation's very purpose is to praise Him!

It's pretty mysterious and perplexing to picture a twinkling star
or a breaking wave praising God. Our earthly minds cannot comprehend what this looks like, but we can trust that it is happening
(see also Isaiah 44:23; Habakkuk 3:3; and Revelation 5:13). All
around us the world is lifting a shout of thanks to our God! Maybe
it's a thunderclap, a rustling wind, a birdsong, or a lion's roar. The
universe's praise is a pattern throughout Scripture, the response to
God's creative works.

When we think back on the creation account in Genesis 1 once again, we see that no element of God's glorious creation is described as created "in His image" until He formed humanity (v. 26). The maple trees, the craggy mountaintops, the heavenly beings—they praise the Lord without the added joy of being made like Him. We were created uniquely, remarkably in His own image—given exceptional dignity, worth, and purpose that the rest of creation just doesn't have. As those created in God's image, we have a unique opportunity to praise Him for the way He's crafted us as individuals, each a different reflection of His character. Whether you pray, journal, dance, take a long walk, knit, or paint, take time to praise our creative God today!

EMBRACING WHOLENESS

I am a unique creation of God, crafted in His image. I praise Him for His faithful work in my life.

23

Deborah, the Leader

Now Deborah, a prophet, the wife of Lappidoth, was leading
Israel at that time. She held court under the Palm of Deborah
between Ramah and Bethel in the hill country of Ephraim, and
the Israelites went up to her to have their disputes decided.

JUDGES 4:4–5 NIV

What does body confidence look like in others? You may admire friends or family who are far more outspoken about their relationship with their body than you are, or you might follow women online who have made self-love their brand, their main message. But for most of us, endeavoring to treat our body as beloved, made in the image of God, is just one aspect of who we are. The truth is, we may not be ready to tell the world we are trying to heal. We still have to go to work, take care of others, do laundry, and eat something other than ice cream for dinner. And while not everyone who has a good relationship with their body shouts it from the rooftops, many who have positive self-esteem lead with an air of confidence, a reassurance that they know who they are. Deborah was one such woman.

Of course, Deborah's relationship with her body is uncertain. But here's what we do know: Deborah was a judge (the only female judge described in the book of Judges), a leader in Israel. She was wise, discerning, and bold. To be a leader, she had to be confident and self-assured. We see this in Judges 4 when Deborah instructed Barak to go to battle with Sisera, and as a result, the people experienced forty years of peace (see Judges 5:31). In fact, in Judges 5 Deborah praised God, saying:

> Hear this, you kings! Listen, you rulers!
> I, even I, will sing to the Lord;
> I will praise the Lord, the God of Israel, in
>   song. (v. 3 NIV)

Deborah had a grounded and steady faith in God, and she unequivocally got her calling and her confidence from the Lord.

We look to the Bible for examples of self-assured, fearless women. Deborah is a wonderful example. While the details of her life are largely unknown, we can affirm that she was a confident leader who relied on God. Deborah was daring and courageous, and people took her seriously. May it be the same for us.

EMBRACING WHOLENESS

Deborah was a confident, amazing woman. May I look to her example as I heal my relationship with my body and come to terms more fully with who I am.

24

For Bad Body Image Days

The LORD your God is with you, the Mighty Warrior who
saves. He will take great delight in you; in his love he will no
longer rebuke you, but will rejoice over you with singing.

ZEPHANIAH 3:17 NIV

Even the most confident person on the planet is going to have
days when they feel uncomfortable or insecure in their body,
days where they don't love—let alone like—the skin they're in.
Perhaps you are just beginning your journey of accepting and respecting your body, and most days you don't have a positive outlook of
yourself. Or maybe you are further along in this endeavor, and your
bad body image days are becoming fewer and fewer. Wherever you
are today in healing your relationship with your body, remember
that it is okay to have days when you don't feel as if you're making
significant progress or huge improvements in your mindset or your
view of your body. You are not failing or inhibiting healing. You are
simply human.

When we face discouragement, off days, or intrusive negative
thoughts about our body, our response is really important. When
we view our negative thoughts as facts and embrace harmful thought
patterns, we become convinced that our relationship with our body
will never change. Every time we give in to these lies, we find them
easier to believe. But, if we see these bad days as simply that—one
bad day in the span of a week, a month, a lifetime—we will find
that we can extend far more grace to ourselves and to the ups and

downs of our relationship with our own body. God never promises we won't have hard times, but He does promise that He will be with us when we face opposition or encounter suffering. As today's verse explains, even when we are in the thick of a bad body image day, God is actively delighting in us, seeing us as His beloved whom He rejoices over.

Bad days are just pit stops on the road to healing. They do not define you. And they don't mean you are doing anything wrong. If you're having one of these days, grappling with the truth that your body is good, may you remember that God is your Creator and companion, a reliable presence that banishes shame. He will walk alongside you through this day and on your path toward growth.

EMBRACING WHOLENESS

A bad body image day does not define me. I can show myself grace as I reject the lies I am tempted to believe about my body.

25

No Quick Fixes

Heal me, LORD, and I will be healed; save me,
and I will be saved, for you are my praise.

JEREMIAH 17:14 CSB

"Lose 20 pounds in 2 months!"

"Take years off your face with this new innovative cream!"

"Curb sugar cravings forever with just one pill a day!"

The beauty and diet industries thrive on big promises and easy fixes. It's much easier to buy a new serum, diet plan, or workout video than to focus on addressing the deep and lasting body insecurity that often drives our purchasing—and they know that. There will always be a new miracle drug, a celebrity-endorsed program, or a trendy new exercise. And when we equate an outward-appearance transformation with a healed inner narrative, the appeal of these products and advertisements that prey on our insecurities is tempting. But, when it comes to your body confidence journey, there are no quick fixes. You can't will your way to loving your body. And you can't shortcut past your trauma and find immediate relief. Embracing the person reflected in the mirror is a process of gradual healing and hard-fought transformation. And while the longer path toward body acceptance may look daunting, accepting and enjoying the journey brings a deeper and more lasting healing than any quick fix ever could.

Long-term healing and transformation are at odds with instant results. Many of us believe deep down that quickly dropping a few pounds, instantly smoothing out our skin, or removing our impulse to overeat would only help our body confidence issues. While it's true that these things may give us a temporary self-esteem boost, we'll find ourselves back in that same spot sooner rather than later, looking for the next quick fix to ease our self-loathing. This is no way to live: giving our money to solve surface problems while advertising points to our next "problem area" as soon as they cash our check. Instead, when we are brave enough to look inward and process the core lies at the heart of our body shame or insecurity, we have a greater opportunity for lasting healing.

When we base our body love in our status as image bearers of the one true God, when we see ourselves as worthy because we are loved by Him, and when we take steps to recognize and reject cultural messaging in favor of biblical truth, we rebuild our relationship with our body. This process might include therapy, reading books on body confidence, or listening to sermons about your body. This self-love journey isn't a quick fix, but it is a worthy pursuit of the wholeness God desires for you.

EMBRACING WHOLENESS

My journey toward body confidence will take however long it takes. God is with me, and the healing is worth it.

26

Defined by Him

Man does not live on bread alone but on every word
that comes from the mouth of the LORD.

DEUTERONOMY 8:3 CSB

Our culture constantly tells us who we are. It tells us to focus on what's wrong with us, what needs to be improved. It tells us we are hard to love, that we are difficult to be around. It tries to define us, discouraging us and keeping us right where we are. These are all lies! Instead, let's remind ourselves today what the Lord says about us and to us, what "comes from the mouth of the LORD" (Deuteronomy 8:3 CSB).

He says:

- You are never alone (Isaiah 41:10).

  God will never leave you. Even when you face times of loneliness and fear, He is right there beside you. He is your Comforter.

- You are complete and whole in Him (Colossians 2:10).

  You are not deficient; you were not created wrong. You are not lacking anything, and you are beloved just as you are.

- You are forgiven (1 John 2:12).

  You are not, and have never been, beyond God's forgiveness. Nothing you can do will change this.

- You are accepted (Romans 15:7).

  Christ does not reject you; He receives you. Even if you have faced rejection in the past, you will not face it in your relationship with Him.

- You are healed (Psalm 30:2).

  As He walks alongside you in your pain, Christ is also a healer. You are not your wounds, your illness, or your situation.

- You have the strength to face your trials (Romans 8:37).

  In this life you will face difficult situations and seasons, but you are empowered by God to persevere. God describes you as a conqueror.

- You are safe and secure in Christ (Colossians 3:3).

  Through your relationship with Christ, you have secured eternity in heaven. Not only that, but you are safe to be who you are in the present moment. Your security does not lie in this world.

When we work to replace the lies trying to infiltrate our heart with these truths, we are reminded just what being created in His image means. Today, pick one of these affirmations and commit it to memory. You are defined by God, not by the world.

EMBRACING WHOLENESS

I am defined by the unchanging truth of Christ's love and acceptance, not by the constantly evolving standards of the world around me. I am whole in Christ.

27

Caring for Your Body

So whether you eat or drink or whatever you
do, do it all for the glory of God.

1 CORINTHIANS 10:31 NIV

No one in your life knows your body like you do. When you have
a bad headache, when you have a knee that's bothering you, or
when you feel self-conscious while dealing with what you consider
a bad breakout, no one understands exactly how you feel. We try
to relate to others' bodily experiences by remembering our own
similar circumstances. But someone else's experiences are largely
unknown to us because we only know our bodies. Each one of us
lives in a different body, so we take care of our body in different
ways. This is okay, even good.

Only you know what it means to care for your body well. Some
of us feel best when we walk a couple times a week and take a
power nap every day, while others feel most comfortable in their
body when they go to the gym each day and have therapy once a
week. Healthy, fit, full, content: these all feel different from body
to body. Oftentimes, however, when we find something that works
for our body, we want to tell others about it. We must be careful
not to force our definition of what it looks like to care for our body
onto other people, steering clear of judging their decisions. When
we remember that we each know our body best, we can meet each
other with compassion instead of judgment.

Others of us haven't even figured out what combination of physical, mental, and emotional health care make our bodies feel best, and we too should be met with grace and understanding. We are all on a journey with our bodies, a unique path that deserves to be met with kindness from others. When we see our bodies as a reflection of God Himself, we can focus on treating ourselves well in order to glorify Him. Even if those around you aren't treating their bodies as you would like, remind yourself that you don't know what their relationships with their bodies are like, and you don't know what their bodies might be going through.

EMBRACING WHOLENESS

I know my body best, and caring for my body might look different than it does for someone else. That's okay! I can glorify God in my own way as I care for myself.

28

Self-Compassion

Therefore, as God's chosen ones, holy and dearly loved, put on
compassion, kindness, humility, gentleness, and patience . . .
COLOSSIANS 3:12 CSB

We are our own worst critics. We talk to ourselves using words that we wouldn't dare speak to a random stranger, let alone our closest friends. Some of us tell ourselves we are falling behind, failing at our career or in our relationships, or aren't good enough for a promotion or a new experience that pushes us out of our comfort zone, like a book club or a Bible study. We beat ourselves up in all manner of ways, creating a narrative that perfection is the standard. But today's verse provides a better way. As Paul, the writer of Colossians, explains—we are to be people of compassion, kindness, humility, gentleness, and patience (Colossians 3:12). Not only can we pray to demonstrate these qualities in our relationships with others, but we can look inwardly and give ourselves the same compassion and care.

Dr. Kristin Neff, an influential psychologist, defines self-compassion this way: "Instead of mercilessly judging and criticizing yourself for various inadequacies or shortcomings, self-compassion means you are kind and understanding when confronted with your failings—after all, who ever said you were supposed to be perfect?"[11] Also, when you take care of yourself, you emulate the love and grace God Himself extends to you. Remember, God created you in His image! He has never seen you as too sinful, too far gone to be loved, or too broken to be held—and He never will. Can you show yourself the same compassion?

Today, we read in verse 12 that we can "put on" compassion, kindness, humility, gentleness, and patience when we interact with others, and we can show these same loving acts to ourselves. This could start by asking God to help you notice your inner critic more, the voice that meets your actions with harsh rebuke instead of gentle love. It could mean becoming more aware of yourself through journaling, therapy, or time alone with your thoughts. Whatever the journey to greater self-compassion looks like for you, may it show you just how loved you are.

EMBRACING WHOLENESS

As someone created in God's image, I am worthy of love. I can show myself more compassion even in my failings, knowing that I am who God says I am.

29

Esther, the Courageous

If you keep quiet at a time like this, deliverance and
relief for the Jews will arise from some other place, but
you and your relatives will die. Who knows if perhaps
you were made queen for just such a time as this?

ESTHER 4:14

We often focus on the second half of Esther's story, probably because it's so redemptive. But when we rush too quickly to the ending, we miss just how big a sacrifice Esther made. Esther was thrown into a horrific situation—kidnapped from her hometown, transported to a new city, chosen by the king, and forced to marry without any regard to what she wanted. Hardship was coming at her from all angles. Yet even when a nightmare became her reality, we see her act with courage, leaning on the sustaining presence of God.

When Esther was chosen to join the harem of young women from throughout the land in the running for queen, she left behind her hopes and dreams of a "normal" family life. If she wasn't chosen to be King Xerxes's queen, she would likely remain in his harem forever as one of his many concubines (see Esther 2). Life as she knew it was over. And once they arrived in this unfamiliar palace, all the women had to subject themselves to an entire year of beauty treatments prior to meeting the king, meant to purify them. Although Esther didn't know the outcome, she had to go through the process. She was likely scared, sad, and confused. Even amidst her pain, God revealed His plan and purpose for her.

Esther's story is more tragic than we are often told. She gave up her plans and hopes for her life when she was selected as a candidate to become queen. She had to sacrifice her body, knowing that if she wasn't chosen by King Xerxes, she would still remain in the palace forever, maybe never even seeing him again. She was thrown into a life she didn't choose, and probably didn't want. For this we can lament. Yet, at the same time, we see God working, even here. Through Esther's courage, her people, the Jews, were delivered from the evil Haman's plot to destroy them. God equipped Esther to save the Jews. She demonstrated a courage that can only be rooted in Him. Esther's story is tragic—that's a fact. Yet her courage in this tragedy is also a truth we cannot ignore.

EMBRACING WHOLENESS

The story of Esther gives me courage. Even when I face unimaginable circumstances, God sustains and empowers me. I do not have to ignore my pain to see God at work.

30

Our Healer

My soul, bless the LORD, and do not forget all his
benefits. He forgives all your iniquity; he heals all
your diseases. He redeems your life from the Pit; he
crowns you with faithful love and compassion.

PSALM 103:2–4 CSB

Sometimes what happens to your body is out of your control.
You catch a cold during your busiest season at work, you gain or
lose weight because of a medication change or an ongoing illness, or
you have an accident that limits your movement in a way you didn't
see coming. Living in a body that can be unpredictable and so very
human is hard, and accepting your body
in all its forms and in its irregular nature
can be even harder.

The good news is that God hasn't
asked us to love ourselves despite our
fickle and frail bodies, but to love ourselves because we are His, created intentionally in our bodies, and He promises
to work for our good in all things (see
Romans 8:28). After all, we live in a
fallen world where everything is affected
by sin, including our bodies. But Jesus
died to redeem us, to heal us. Although you may not experience a
miraculous healing, a speedy recovery, or a dramatic transformation

> The good news is that
> God hasn't asked
> us to love ourselves
> despite our fickle
> and frail bodies, but
> to love ourselves
> because we are His.

in this life, God is still your healer—bringing long lasting restoration to your life through a relationship with Him.

When what is happening to our bodies feels out of our control, our first defense is prayer. Numerous instances throughout Scripture show us that God can completely heal us, no matter how complicated and confusing our case (see Jeremiah 17:14; Psalm 41:3; Isaiah 38:16–17). But God doesn't promise a full bodily restoration, and sometimes we don't experience the healing we crave. While prolonged body discomfort, illness, or injury is no doubt discouraging and even isolating, it does not mean God hasn't heard your prayers or that He isn't with you. You are still held by Him, even here. We don't know why God chooses to heal some bodies and not others, but we do know that healing is more than skin deep.

Even as we long for a body that feels predictable and safe, we know we can experience mental, emotional, and spiritual healing through Him. Through spending time in prayer, reading Scripture, and surrounding ourselves with people who point us to Jesus, we can find a healing we didn't even expect. As 2 Corinthians 4:16 (CSB) says, "Therefore we do not give up. Even though our outer person is being destroyed, our inner person is being renewed day by day." We may not have control, but we have Jesus—and what can be better than that?

EMBRACING WHOLENESS

When my body feels out of my control, I can look to Jesus as my Comforter and my Healer.

31

Living as an Advocate

Speak up for those who cannot speak for themselves;
ensure justice for those being crushed. Yes, speak up for
the poor and helpless, and see that they get justice.

PROVERBS 31:8–9

Whether we have millions in the bank or we don't know where our next meal is coming from—whether our calendar is full of social engagements or we feel forgotten or unloved—we are all made in the image of God. Nothing can sway how God sees us: not our own human effort, not our social status, not our Instagram following. We are part of the imago Dei (image of God) family. And as believers, we are all one in Jesus Christ (Galatians 3:28).

Today's passage calls us to be advocates, knowing that we are united with others because they too are created by God for special and exceptional purposes. An advocate is someone who defends, supports, promotes, or pleads for a cause, a group, or another person.[12] The Bible talks frequently about advocating for the poor: both the widowed and the orphaned that we may not know or be in frequent contact with (see Proverbs 29:7 and James 1:27) and those close to us. For example, Leviticus 25:35 (ESV) says: "If your brother becomes poor and cannot maintain himself with you, you shall support him as though he were a stranger and a sojourner, and he shall live with you." When we support those around us, not only will we find ourselves encouraged, but our community will grow. United under the banner of imago Dei, our advocacy gains potency.

Advocacy begins with empathy and understanding. Although we may not be in a similar situation as someone else, we can pray and ask questions, trying more deeply to understand where the other person is and what they may need. When we listen to understand and act to meet the needs of others, we become their advocate. We learn to love our neighbor better. As Billy Graham once said, "Just thinking of and serving with others can be an antidote to negative and unhealthy introspection."[13]

EMBRACING WHOLENESS

I commit to being an advocate, using my voice and my actions, along with my prayers, to help others when I see a need.

32

Body and Soul

When God created mankind, he made
them in the likeness of God.

GENESIS 5:1 NIV

One inch of your skin has approximately nineteen million skin cells.[14] Your brain processes about seventy thousand thoughts a day.[15] One school of thought believes that the emotions you feel are electrochemical signals that are released in your brain and flow through you in an unending cycle.[16] In short, you are amazing! Every freckle on your arm, the way you think through difficult situations, the settled feeling you feel in your spirit after doing something you love—every single aspect of you was created in the image, or likeness, of God. You are complex, complicated, and astonishingly unique. You are the imago Dei: body and soul.

Let's distinguish these aspects of your being. Your body, your physical being, is the easiest part of you to understand. It reflects the amazing humanness of Christ. When Jesus was born as a baby, He chose to experience the humanity of His creation. Jesus had moments when His body felt weak, when He knew He needed rest. He also surely had times when He was bursting with energy, His body ready for a full day of walking, preaching, and ministering. We live in a different time, yes, but our bodies can still reflect Christ and His experience as a person. We can honor our bodies that were created by God by treating them with respect. We can rest in the fact that Christ knows what it's like to have a physical body that sometimes feels comfortable and sometimes lets you down.

Second, you can think of your soul as the way you commune with God. In Scripture, "spirit" and "soul" are often used to mean the same thing, the immaterial part of you that can never fade.[17] If you are a follower of Christ, your soul is also uniquely integrated with the Holy Spirit. Your soul is not physical, but rather the essence of who you are. Although our bodies will die, our souls will live on forever (2 Corinthians 5:8), and your feelings are intrinsically linked to your unbreakable soul. The fruit of the Spirit, as we see in Galatians 5:22–23, is love, joy, peace, forbearance, kindness, goodness, faithfulness, gentleness and self-control. You are a complex, multifaceted, and beautifully intricate person *and* you were made in His image: body and soul.

EMBRACING WHOLENESS

Every part of who I am was crafted by God with intention and love.

33

Nurturing God's Creation

The earth is the LORD's, and everything in it. The
world and all its people belong to him.

PSALM 24:1

Our planet is so diverse, full of jungle cats slinking through thick
underbrush, camels traversing sandy dunes, beetles smaller
than a pinhead scurrying up thick trees in search of food. In fact,
unique ecosystems exist on this earth: tundra, coniferous forest,
temperate deciduous forest, rainforest, grassland, shrubland, and
desert.[18] Within each of these ecosystems live thousands of different species of animals, insects, and vegetation. The Lord created
them all! Everything from the vibrant poison dart frog of Central
and South America, to the chill capybara of South America, to the
other-worldly narwhals in the Arctic Ocean—all are crafted by and
are cared for by God Himself.

We have the opportunity, as those created in God's image, to
partner with God by intentionally caring for this vast and beautiful creation today. Recycling and living a more sustainable lifestyle
provide two simple ways to do this. According to the UN: "Plastic
waste can take anywhere from 20 to 500 years to decompose, and
even then, it never fully disappears; it just gets smaller and smaller."[19]
Maybe start by taking plastic and cardboard to your local recycling
center, buying in bulk when you can, and opting for reusable contain-
ers. Buy clothing from thrift stores or more sustainable companies
instead of opting for fast fashion. Give back to nonprofits that care

for endangered species. Volunteer at your local humane society. You don't need a perfect pursuit of sustainability to honor God and His creation with your time and money.

As humans, we have a responsibility to care for creation as the Lord does. We are created in His image after all, and He delights in us honoring Him in this way. Revelation 4:11 explains:

> You are worthy, O Lord our God,
>> to receive glory and honor and power.
> For you created all things,
>> and they exist because you created
>> what you pleased.

We glorify God when we care for our diverse and magnificent planet in intentional ways.

EMBRACING WHOLENESS

I am a part of God's creation, and I have the ability to treat the earth with the respect it deserves. God creates good things, of which I am a part.

34

Mary, the Faithful

And Mary said: "My soul glorifies the Lord, and my spirit rejoices in God my Savior, for he has been mindful of the humble state of his servant. From now on all generations will call me blessed, for the Mighty One has done great things for me—holy is his name."

LUKE 1:46–49 NIV

Mary wins the award for receiving the biggest surprise of anyone, ever. Not only did she find out she was pregnant, which was already seemingly impossible because she was a virgin, but she was pregnant with the Messiah. No surprise birthday party or vacation, unexpected promotion or job loss, or even unforeseen pregnancy can top that. And while there is little doubt that Mary was shocked by the news, her first reaction was one of joyful acceptance. Her response to the angel Gabriel and her willingness to fulfill this extraordinary calling exemplified unwavering faith and submission to God's will. She responded to the news with: "I am the Lord's servant. . . . May your word to me be fulfilled" (Luke 1:38 NIV). Wow.

Jesus, the Son of Man, grew and developed in her womb, in her very body. Mary almost certainly experienced morning sickness, swollen ankles, exhaustion, and cravings. Her body changed and grew with her pregnancy, accommodating the miracle happening within her. As we look to partner with our own bodies, building trust with and love for ourselves, we look to the example of Mary, who faithfully responded to the life-changing call of God with praise. While Mary likely had moments of fear, anxiety, and even self-consciousness as she explained to others that her baby was a product of the Holy Spirit, her reaction recorded in Scripture is one of awe, wonder, and thanks. Today's passage is only a section of Mary's song in Luke 1, nine verses where Mary worships the Lord not only for what He had done in her life, but for what He had done for her people through the generations. May we react the same way when God does a mighty work in us.

As we work on our relationship with our body, may we have courage to place our trust in God alone. We do not always know how He is working, and sometimes it will surprise us, but we do know He is working for our good (Romans 8:28). Mary, the mother of Jesus, partnered with God with her very body. She is an inspiration to us of faithfulness, humility, and great love for the Lord.

EMBRACING WHOLENESS

God has done great things for me, and He will continue to fulfill His promises.

35

Beyond Looks

Humans do not see what the LORD sees, for humans
see what is visible, but the LORD sees the heart.

1 SAMUEL 16:7 CSB

We're all familiar with the saying "Don't judge a book by its cover." This is much easier said than done. Have you ever found yourself in a destructive pattern where your worth comes from comparing your outward appearance to others, judging yourself against them either to boost your self-confidence or affirm your negative self-talk? When we judge others based on their outward appearance and use this as a tool of comparison, we are leveraging the goodness of their creation for our own personal gain. Like us, they are people made in God's image. If we put unnecessary emphasis on the importance of looks, we are also not cultivating community with our fellow image bearers.

As today's passage explains, the Lord looks not at the visible (outward appearance) but at the heart (the core of who we are). In a similar way, we can emulate God by retraining our brains to see outward appearance as part of the imago Dei instead of as a tool for comparison. When we do this, we deemphasize the competitiveness of outward appearance and reorient our priorities with those of the Lord. When we look for God in others, we see beyond competition and comparison.

Consider this: Who do you love most in this world? A best friend, a parent or parental figure, a romantic partner? What do you love about them? While there may be something about their appearance that draws you to them, it likely isn't the first, second, or even fifth thing you love! Perhaps it's their kindness toward others, the way they show up for you in difficult times, or their infectious love of life. Not only are these traits unrelated to their outward appearance, but they are also reflections of the heart of God Himself. As those created in God's image, we learn to be kind, faithful, and loving because He is kind, faithful, and loving. When we look at the heart, the motivations, and the innate personality characteristics of others, we are once again reminded of the inherent worth of those around us (see John 7:24).

EMBRACING WHOLENESS

I can look for God in others, knowing that we are all created in His image. Outward appearance isn't the most important thing, and it never will be.

36

A Life of Integrity

I will lead a life of integrity in my own home.

PSALM 102:2

We hear the word *integrity* a lot these days. To explain someone's mental toughness, it's branded across gym T-shirts and on journals; to describe a building or a car's safety and reliability, it's splashed across your television screen; and to remind consumers that a business is honest, it's included in a company's name. As integrity continues to be a buzzword, it can lose meaning for our personal lives. *Merriam-Webster* describes integrity as "total honesty and sincerity."[20] Would you describe yourself in this way? What could it look like to be a person of integrity?

Created in the image of God, you are called to be a person of total honesty and sincerity. Today's verse of Psalm 102:2 takes it one step further though, calling us to "lead a life of integrity *in my own home*" (emphasis mine). This passage makes it personal. Sure, it's important to approach our relationships with friends and family with honesty, reliability, and decency. But the emphasis is even greater when we bring it into our most sacred space, our home. How do we act when no one else is around? Would you describe yourself as motivated by goodness, virtue, and honesty? Or do you act differently when you are alone, knowing that others will never find out the true you?

The pursuit of integrity is not a shameful one. God isn't looking down on you judging you for falling into bad habits or impure behaviors when you are alone in your own home. He meets you only with grace and with love. He is waiting for you to come to Him, growing your integrity through prayer and connection with Him. We can only truly live a life of integrity by centering our life around our relationship with the Lord, coming to Him for strength, perseverance, and hope. After all, He embodies integrity—it's who He is.

EMBRACING WHOLENESS

I can be a person of honesty, reliability, and virtue when I root my life in my relationship with God. God has given me everything I need to be a person of honesty and virtue.

God embodies
integrity—it's
who He is.

37

Becoming like Him

Now may the God of peace himself sanctify you completely.
And may your whole spirit, soul, and body be kept sound
and blameless at the coming of our Lord Jesus Christ.

1 THESSALONIANS 5:23 CSB

W e're tackling a tough theological topic today: sanctification. Don't worry, we'll walk through it together! To set the stage: we were created in the imago Dei, in God's image (Genesis 1:27). As Christians, we don't need to accomplish anything to gain His favor, to be made even more in His likeness. He sees us as loved and created for a purpose—exactly as we are right now (see the example of Jeremiah in Jeremiah 1:5). That is always true. Think of your imago-Dei status as one side of the coin, and this process called sanctification as the other side. Sanctification is the way in which God transforms us into a new person as we learn and grow more in our relationship with Him.

Jim Elliot, as quoted by his wife, Elisabeth Elliot, explained it this way: "One does not surrender a life in an instant. That which is lifelong can only be surrendered in a lifetime."[21] So our sanctification is a lifelong process alongside our Lord and Savior. When sin entered the world, humans were now capable both of being made in His image and marring that image with sin. Sanctification means we can be made more holy, because the more we grow in our faith, the more we are becoming like our Christ, who is holy. Philippians 1:6 (CSB) says: "I am sure of this, that he who started a good work in you will carry it on to completion until the day of Christ Jesus." (For more on sanctification, read Galatians 2:20; 2 Corinthians 5:17; 1 Corinthians 6:11; and Romans 6:6.)

Understanding sanctification is important because it frees us from the pressure to be perfect. It reminds us that God has not called us to be perfect people, but to be sanctified people. Of course, if you have a personal relationship with God, you are redeemed! Christ died on the cross for your redemption. But you will still stumble; you will still make mistakes. So, sanctification teaches us to be people who come to Him, knowing that our continuous growth toward Christ will refine and refashion us in the best way. The more we grow toward Christ, the more our hearts are changed. We are each a work in progress, becoming more like Him through sanctification.

EMBRACING WHOLENESS

With each day, I am becoming more like Christ. As I grow in my relationship with Him, I am being made new.

38

The Woman at the Well

The woman said, "I know that Messiah" (called Christ) "is coming. When he comes, he will explain everything to us." Then Jesus declared, "I, the one speaking to you—I am he."

JOHN 4:25–26 NIV

Our body often carries the shame, blame, and guilt of our regrets. Perhaps it's a physical scar from a teenage prank gone wrong or a childish game that was more dangerous than it appeared. Or it feels like a deeper emotional scar that reminds us of a time we used our body to express anger, lust, or sadness that we want to take back or forget. The woman at the well, a Samaritan woman, knew this type of wound well. She was an outcast from society, and she likely carried that shame with her wherever she went. She even traveled to the well in the heat of the day to avoid having to interact with others. There she met Jesus. He knew her past, her mistakes, her embarrassment—and He loved her all the same. In fact, Jesus revealed His true identity as the Messiah of the world for the first time to this woman. Jesus came to redeem all of us—body, mind, and soul.

In John 4, we read that Jesus addressed the woman personally: "Everyone who drinks this water will be thirsty again, but whoever drinks the water I give them will never thirst. Indeed, the water I give them will become in them a spring of water welling up to eternal life" (vv. 13–14 NIV). Like the Samaritan woman, if we want true healing, true forgiveness, true renewal, Jesus is the only answer. He is the living water. He redeemed this fractured woman, and He offers this same redemption to you two thousand years later. There is nothing you have done, there is nothing that you carry, there is no burden too big for God. As we see in this story, Jesus not only knows your past but accepts you in the present. As you work toward a life free from body shame, release your burdens into His arms today and be refreshed by the living water He offers in return.

After her encounter with Jesus, this woman left her water jar behind and ran to tell others about the One who knew everything about her yet loved her unconditionally. When we know Jesus and experience His healing touch in our own lives, we cannot help but tell others. As you experience healing in your relationship with your own body through Jesus, may you tell others of the One who made you whole again.

EMBRACING WHOLENESS

Jesus knows everything about me, and He loves me deeply and unconditionally. He can bring healing to my relationship with my body even today.

39

The Privilege of Aging

I will be your God throughout your lifetime— until
your hair is white with age. I made you, and I will
care for you. I will carry you along and save you.

ISAIAH 46:4 NLT

The anti-aging industry is projected to produce sales of 81.7
billion dollars in 2025.[22] Many people get painful injections or
surgeries to look younger; others use expensive creams, serums, and
oils; and still others try an ever-changing array of vitamins or pills.
While these aren't inherently bad things, they do hint at a bigger
problem—we fear aging. Whether we worry about declining beauty,
deteriorating health, or diminished relevance, our culture teaches
us to fear a process God Himself created. Instead of investing our
dollars in products that, best-case scenario, will only slightly prolong
the inevitable, what if we embraced the process and put aside fear,
knowing that aging is a privilege?

The sobering truth is that not everyone gets to age. And while
aging does come with new aches and pains, it also comes with a
plethora of blessings. As we age, we learn more about ourselves and
about others. We have more opportunities to deepen our faith: to ask
questions, to investigate, and to grow in God. We have more chances
to travel, to find new hobbies, to have fun! Our hair may turn white,
and our bodies may expand, but our wisdom and experience will
grow right alongside these changes. Aging won't always be grace-
ful, but it is a beautiful process. Even as you change throughout the

years, your identity will remain rooted in God's image. As God says in today's verse, you will be carried by Him year after year.

I'm not saying you should immediately throw away your anti-aging face cream or stop building up your physical stamina. However, it's worth considering how much energy you are investing into fighting the natural aging process. What if, instead, you invested that energy into liking your life and absorbing all the blessings God's given you for as long as you have here on this earth? Aging is a privilege, and nothing is better than walking year by year alongside your eternal Creator.

EMBRACING WHOLENESS

I don't have to fear aging, but instead can embrace the process of growth and change throughout each year, each day, each moment.

40

Seeing Yourself as You Are

Let's examine and probe our ways, and turn back to the LORD.

LAMENTATIONS 3:40 CSB

Do you find yourself fixating on aspects of your appearance for hours, days, or even weeks on end, unable to distance yourself from your dissatisfaction? Have you allowed your negativity toward your body to impact your interactions with others? No, this isn't the start of a sales pitch, but it could be a sign of body dysmorphia. Many people suffer from some form of body dysmorphia, a distorted view of our body that causes us to see it as different than it actually is. We may think we are bigger, less attractive, or less composed than we are, which causes us to continually believe lies about our body and how the world perceives it. To see our body inaccurately and accept that inaccurate interpretation as truth robs us of the bodily joy and peace God intends for us. It can lead to a relentless cycle of self-criticism, comparison, and despair. And when we utilize our negative perceptions as fuel for our body hatred, our body confidence is squelched before it can even begin to grow.

As the Good News Translation of Proverbs 4:23 warns: "Be careful how you think; your life is shaped by your thoughts." Breaking agreements with the lies we have thought and accepted about our own body, the distorted view we have mistakenly accepted as truth, is pivotal to the self-love journey. And it starts with identifying the lies you have believed about your body. When did you start thinking that your acne deemed you as unacceptable? Why do you believe you are heavier than you actually are? When did you start spending much of your day fixating on the size of your thighs or your stomach? When we bravely confront our own body dysmorphia and untrue perceptions of ourselves, then we are able to find room for compassion, respect, and even love.

God longs for you to see your body accurately so you can accept it in all its goodness. When we know and understand our own body more deeply, we are able to understand that this body, as it is right now, was made by God in love, reflecting His image. When you see your body as it truly is—and receive that your body is good—this acceptance, peace, and freedom will overflow into other areas of your life.

EMBRACING WHOLENESS

God is with me, and He will help me to identify and find freedom from my body dysmorphic beliefs. This is an important step toward healing.

41

The Work of the Holy Spirit

But the Advocate, the Holy Spirit, whom the Father
will send in my name, will teach you all things and
will remind you of everything I have said to you.

JOHN 14:26 NIV

Have you ever had one of those "gut-feeling" moments? Maybe you were about to sign a lease on a new apartment, but something felt off and unsettled. Or perhaps you are having coffee with a friend, and you realize they've hurt your feelings and you need to talk it through. Or it could be as simple as scrolling through social media and realizing just how much time you've been spending comparing yourself to others. Some describe this as an intuition, a hunch, or instinct. As a follower of Jesus Christ, your gut feelings often originate with the Holy Spirit's promptings.

Your gut feelings often originate with the Holy Spirit's promptings.

When we follow the Lord, the Holy Spirit comes to us and continually works within us. We increasingly begin to realize that many of our gut feelings are actually the Holy Spirit at work. As today's verse explains, Jesus sent us the Holy Spirit to be our advocate. This means He is our steady support, always there to defend and to comfort. It can be confusing to reckon with the fact that the Holy Spirit lives inside of us, but if you think of it as that guiding voice, it's sometimes easier to wrap your mind around. He is constantly teaching us by leading us closer to the path God has prepared for us.

He is our helper, elsewhere described in the Bible as wisdom (Ephesians 1:17), power and love (2 Timothy 1:7), and grace (Hebrews 10:29), among others. The amazing thing about the Holy Spirit is that we can ask His help in understanding Him more fully! We can turn to Him in prayer, asking for a heightened awareness of His leading. And when we take the Holy Spirit at His word, consulting that intuitive feeling inside and praying for guidance, we often make decisions we can feel more at peace with in the long run. We are made in the image of God, which includes the image of the Holy Spirit. He is there for you, and He wants to help you, guide you, and give you peace.[23]

EMBRACING WHOLENESS

The Holy Spirit lives within me! I can listen to His leading with confidence, knowing that God is at work in my life, and He knows what I need.

42

Advocating for Yourself

Physical training is good, but training for godliness is much better, promising benefits in this life and in the life to come.

1 TIMOTHY 4:8

You can physically train your body to get stronger, build endurance, or become more flexible. You can join a gym, hire a personal trainer, or purchase a new workout program. This type of training can be a great tool for learning to love your body (see devotion 49 on joyful movement), but today's verse says that a different kind of training is preferred, a training in godliness. (Hmm, I've never seen godliness training advertised on social media or a flyer in the gym for a godliness program!) What does being a student of godliness look like? It certainly includes growing your relationship with God through studying Scripture, praying, and surrounding yourself with Christian community. It is also linked to the work of the Holy Spirit inside you, connecting you to your body and helping you advocate for yourself.

Training in godliness reframes your thoughts, aligning all your decisions with the Holy Spirit. Paul in Ephesians 4 calls this "put[ting] off your old self" (v. 22 NIV). And perhaps your old self, also translated as your "old way of life" in the New Living Translation, treated your body with disgust, trying to shame your body into being different, or ignoring it altogether. Later in this passage, Paul tells us "to put on the new self, created to be like God in true righteousness and holiness" (v. 24 NIV). This new self, constantly growing and learning with the help of the Holy Spirit, values your body, acknowledges your inherent dignity and beauty, and speaks up for yourself. God desires for you to be connected with your body—physically, emotionally, mentally, spiritually. After all, it is the home of His Holy Spirit (1 Corinthians 6:19). God is training you up, and His Holy Spirit can empower you to speak up for yourself as an act of self-love.

Advocating for yourself and your body can take a lot of different shapes and forms, all important. It can look like speaking up or clarifying your point of view if you feel unheard or misunderstood. Or removing yourself from a situation where you feel uncomfortable, either physically or emotionally. Or like boldly seeking out help or support if you are being mistreated in any way. God created you in His image, and He desires for you to be heard, respected, and understood. Your body matters—you matter. God is at work in you, and His Holy Spirit can empower you to make choices that honor Him and respect you. Second Corinthians 3:17 says, "For the Lord is the Spirit, and wherever the Spirit of the Lord is, there is freedom." You can advocate for yourself, knowing that you are supported by a God who loves you more than you can imagine.

EMBRACING WHOLENESS

I am being trained up in godliness, and advocating for myself is a part of that training. I can speak up for myself knowing that the Holy Spirit is always with me.

43

For When Your Body Fails

The LORD is the strength of his people, a
fortress of salvation for his anointed one.

PSALM 28:8 NIV

I f you haven't figured it out yet, your body will fail you. It will get
sick, tired, or chemically imbalanced. Your journey with your body
may include chronic illness, disability, or mental health issues. It
can be hard to appreciate your body when you just don't feel good.
Something as temporary as a sinus infection or a stomach bug can
be enough to knock us out and make us doubt the goodness of our
body. Something like an autoimmune disease can completely distance
us from the respect and love we have for our body. Understanding
our worth as an embodied person created in God's image is a process, and it's okay if we face setbacks and discouragement when our
body just doesn't seem to be working properly. Even as you sit with
these valid feelings about your failing body, be encouraged that the
weakness of your body also presents a very real opportunity to find
your strength in God alone.

Theologian J. I. Packer explains it this way: "God uses chronic
pain and weakness, along with other afflictions, as his chisel for
sculpting our lives. Felt weakness deepens dependence on Christ
for strength each day. The weaker we feel, the harder we lean. And
the harder we lean, the stronger we grow spiritually, even while
our bodies waste away."[24] While it can be difficult to turn to God
in prayer when our body fails us, when we do, we find a source

of reliable and unbending strength waiting for us there. He is a fortress, a stronghold who provides both protection and comfort. Especially when our body is feeling sick and our spirit is low, we need our Comforter. He will never fail us, even when our body does.

Whether your illness is temporary or lifelong, you are still created in the image of God: you are loved, you are safe, and you are strengthened in Him. Second Corinthians 1:10 (NIV) explains, "He has delivered us from such a deadly peril, and he will deliver us again. On him we have set our hope that he will continue to deliver us." Let God, your Father, be your source of strength and your Deliverer today, no matter how your body feels.

EMBRACING WHOLENESS

My body will fail me, but my Lord never will. He is my strength today.

44

Freedom through the Spirit

For the Lord is the Spirit, and wherever the
Spirit of the Lord is, there is freedom.

2 CORINTHIANS 3:17

Can you recall the last time you felt truly free? A moment when you felt uninhibited, when you couldn't think of anything that weighed you down? You likely felt light, unbothered, and maybe even joyful. In the moment, you may not have described the feeling as "freedom." When you experience a moment of relief and lightness like this, it's so good that you want to bottle it up and release it little by little each day. Some people experience freedom by getting out in nature, taking a deep breath while camping under the stars. Others feel true freedom while traveling, the experience of other cultures opening their horizons in new and exciting ways. Some feel freedom when they engage in a hobby that makes their heart sing, like writing, crocheting, cooking, golfing, or fishing.

For many of us, these moments of freedom are rare. When we are mired in the challenges of everyday life, this feeling of freedom is frustratingly difficult to grasp. Today's verse, 2 Corinthians 3:17, reminds us that the Holy Spirit, who dwells inside of us at all times, is freedom Himself. And through Him, we can capture that joyous feeling daily. Praise God! This verse explains that where the Spirit of the Lord is, there is freedom. Wherever He may go, freedom goes there too. Freedom is who He is.

How can we experience this aspect of God's character? By growing in our relationship with the Holy Spirit through prayer. We can ask the Holy Spirit for an extra dose of this freeing feeling, knowing that He is always listening to us. Romans 8:26 explains that even when we don't know what to pray, the Holy Spirit will intercede for us, praying on our behalf. We can ask Him for freedom, even when we don't know exactly what this looks like in our day-to-day life. Galatians 5:13 reminds us that we are called to freedom. Freedom can be a part of who you are too with the help of the Spirit. So let's go after that freedom today! A freedom that will cheer us on, strengthen us for the journey, and comfort us in the hard times.

EMBRACING WHOLENESS

I can live a life of freedom with the help of the Holy Spirit. I was created in the image of God, and God includes the Holy Spirit. As I pray to Him, the Holy Spirit will empower me for the day ahead.

45

Guilt Isn't an Ingredient

Taste and see that the LORD is good. How happy
is the person who takes refuge in him!

PSALM 34:8 CSB

Packaging declares this dried fruit is "guilt-free!," while that friend explains how your favorite ice cream is their "guilty pleasure." The food industry serves up guilt seven days a week, even when all we are trying to do is enjoy some potato chips or try a new brand of peanut butter. Research shows that the average American feels guilt over the consumption of twenty-nine percent of their food, around five times in a given week.[25] The way we associate guilt with food points to a value system that assigns certain foods as "bad" and others as "good." But foods aren't inherently bad or good; they just serve different purposes. Some food helps our eyesight, others strengthen our bones, and still more varieties give us an energy burst. Food delights us, comforts us, or makes us feel nostalgic. All foods fuel us, giving us necessary calories and a variety of nutrients. There is no moral value to food, and guilt is never an ingredient.

God designed food to nourish and sustain us, a truth often lost in the noise of anxieties over health and body image. When we see foods as "good" and "bad" and then proceed to guilt ourselves over "bad" choices, we damage our progress toward body acceptance. More damaging than the food itself is our inner critic. When we allow our inner critic to control our food choices, we completely ignore self-compassion. But hating ourselves and berating our motives will never result in self-love. Rather than viewing food as an enemy that must be battled and conquered, we can see it as a partner in the journey toward caring well for our bodies.

Just as we, as Christians, nurture our souls through praying, reading the Bible, and investing in our relationship with God, we can nurture our bodies with all manner of foods, treating ourselves with the same love and care God bestows upon us. Our God is not a God of guilt and condemnation (see Romans 8:1), so we emulate Him when we release food guilt from our lives. As we do so, we partner with God and take one step closer to healing our relationships with our bodies.

EMBRACING WHOLENESS

I release myself from guilt over my food choices. Instead, I look to God to guide and direct me on my journey to body acceptance.

46

Different Bodies, Different Experiences

We do not dare to classify or compare ourselves
with some who commend themselves. When they
measure themselves by themselves and compare
themselves with themselves, they are not wise.

2 CORINTHIANS 10:12 NIV

Every person's journey with their body is unique because every person is unique. We all grew up in different environments, experienced different ways our parents or caregivers related to their bodies, and had a different relationship with food. While all of us need a little help and healing when it comes to our connection with our body, this will look different from person-to-person. For some of us, part of reconnecting with our body will mean delving into the world of fitness. For others, it will be researching various foods and recipes. And for some, it will look like attending therapy or buying different sized clothes. The tricky part here is that—even though we are likely to experience body liberation in a specific way—we can't expect others to copy us and do exactly what we did. Instead, we can celebrate each other's journeys, even when they look different from our own.

Maybe a friend is embarking on an eating plan you'd never recommend, is working out way more than you would, or is listening to podcasts from people you don't like. But if it's working for her, and she seems to be experiencing genuine growth in her relationship with her body, then it's a win. (As long as she isn't participating in or promoting something harmful.) Celebrating other people's journeys with their bodies doesn't diminish your own experiences or breakthroughs. Instead, it enriches your understanding of the complexity of being a human with a body, building grace and empathy for others in the process. It reminds us that our shared struggles and triumphs extend beyond the surface, that we are all at different places in our relationships with our bodies. It opens lines of communication, creating space to discuss self-esteem and body respect.

Just as we are called to bear one another's burdens (Galatians 6:2), we are also called to rejoice in one another's victories (Romans 12:15), including those victories that involve embracing our bodies. As we navigate our own journeys with our bodies, let's extend the same grace, compassion, and celebration we desire for ourselves to those around us. As we do, we not only mirror Christ but also create a world where everybody is honored and cherished.

EMBRACING WHOLENESS

I celebrate the unique healing journey of others, even when it looks different from my own.

47

God Is for You

*If God is for us, who can ever be against us? Since
he did not spare even his own Son but gave him up
for us all, won't he also give us everything else?*

ROMANS 8:31–32

God is for you. He is working for your good, even when you can't see it right away. Perhaps you've been praying and dreaming for a change, for a new relationship, for financial freedom, or for clarity in your career, and your big prayer isn't being answered as quickly as you'd like. It can be so hard to wait on the Lord, to be patient with His timing. But instead of letting discouragement pull you down, what if you focused on worshiping in the waiting? Author Diane L. Dunton says it this way: "I wait for what comes and experience the joy and delight of the unexpected."[26] There is so much joy to be had in the everyday, in the small ways God is working for you and answering prayers you didn't even know to pray.

When we reorient our minds to focus on how God is with us each and every day, the waiting feels less burdensome. We realize God is at work in the here and now, smiling down upon us while we go throughout our busy days. For example, maybe you breeze through the airport after praying against delays because you have flying anxiety. Or you were nervous about a presentation at work or at school, and you rock it and get a lot of positive feedback. Or, even simpler, maybe you make a shockingly good meal, have a really fun hangout with a pal, or have a restful night in with the family after a busy week. Whatever your day-to-day life looks like, there are so many moments God is working. We often forget that some of these moments are answers to prayers or things we would have only hoped for years, months, or days before.

God wants to bless you, and when we recognize these everyday blessings for what they are, evidence of God at work, it draws us nearer to Him. Romans 8:28 says: "And we know that God causes everything to work together for the good of those who love God and are called according to his purpose for them." God is working for you each and every day. All we have to do is notice His good work. Once we get into a rhythm of worshiping in the waiting, the waiting may seem like the blessing after all.

EMBRACING WHOLENESS

God is for me. Even today, He is working in my life.

48

Living as God's Image Bearers

Don't copy the behavior and customs of this world, but let God transform you into a new person by changing the way you think.

ROMANS 12:2

As you go through your day, you are bombarded with seemingly endless advertisements that tell you who you are. Billboards, commercials, podcast sponsors, ads on social media, pop-up ads on Google, and so much more. Is your head spinning yet? Research shows the average American is exposed to between four thousand and ten thousand ads every single day.[27] And these ads aren't only compelling you to buy something—but even more insidious, they want to cause you to experience a void within yourself that only a product could fill.

Advertisements conflict and confuse, trying to make us feel like we are missing out. They say things like you have "too much time on your hands" and "not enough time in the day." They tell us: "spend more time alone" yet "have deeper friendships." They exhort, "be a minimalist" and "you aren't giving enough money to worthy causes." See the confusion here? If we pay attention to the abundance of conflicting messages, we find ourselves confounded, disheartened, and overcome with feeling both too much and not enough. But there is hope! As we raise our awareness to the potential harm of these advertisements, we can tune out the world's words and turn to our God who offers nothing but peace. Our God is not a God of confusion, not one trying to convince you of your lack.

While advertisements aren't necessarily the "behavior[s] and customs" that Paul (the author of Romans) mentions here, their messages transform our thinking and our behavior if we listen to them. And while recognizing and resisting cultural messaging takes time and self-awareness, today's verse tells us that your transformation is waiting on the other side. The Bible, God's message, tells us we are made in His image (Genesis 1:27), we are free from condemnation (Romans 8:1), and we lack nothing in God, who guides us and cares for us (Psalm 23). Living out our image-bearer status in a world full of noise means investing in our relationship with the Lord. He is the only one who will transform us into a new person. No face cream, productivity app, or meal-kit box can do that.

EMBRACING WHOLENESS

Psalm 23:1 says that with God, I lack nothing. A growing relationship with Him can create clarity and transformation in my life.

49

Joyful Movement

David and all Israel were celebrating with all their
might before the LORD, with castanets, harps,
lyres, timbrels, sistrums and cymbals.

2 SAMUEL 6:5 NIV

Language around exercise motivation is geared toward demanding too much from our bodies, working out solely for the purpose of weight loss or body transformation. And while some people enjoy this type of extreme, push-it-to-the-limits movement, many of us have unknowingly adopted this cultural messaging that the goal of exercise is to punish our bodies and overexert ourselves. There is value in discipline and rigorous training (1 Corinthians 9:27)—especially if you are a competitive athlete. For many of us who struggle with body image, though, exercise becomes a penalty for enjoying food and a hindrance to your self-love journey. Instead of embracing that harmful mindset, we can look to Scripture and listen to our bodies to learn a new, better way—joyful movement. Joyful movement is defined as "a way of approaching physical activity that emphasizes pleasure, choice, flexibility, celebration, and intuition."[28]

David was a big proponent of joyful movement, dancing before the Lord on many occasions and "with all his might" (see also 2 Samuel 6:14). As we see through David's example, joyful movement can be an act of praise to God, an expression of worship where we don't need to worry about appearances or skill. Psalm 149:3 (NIV), which David wrote, echoes this sentiment saying, "Let them praise his name with dancing and make music to him with timbrel and harp." We can therefore safely assume that David enjoyed dancing and found pleasure in praising the Lord this way.

What type of movement sounds fun and freeing to you? Perhaps you've always wanted to roller skate, but you were afraid how you'd look cruising about town. Or maybe you love swimming but never take advantage of your time in the pool because your fear of going out in your swimsuit is holding you back. Or maybe you like to walk, to jump rope, to run, or to horseback ride. Joyful movement is personal and is just that—joyful! It's an opportunity to let our body move freely, to release our inhibitions, and even to praise the Lord. You may not find your preferred method of joyful movement right away (and you may fall down once or twice while roller skating), but the joy is also in the process. When we see moving our body as a way to connect with God and to find moments of freedom, we become more aligned with the image of God in which we are made.

EMBRACING WHOLENESS

I have permission to move my body in ways I find fun and freeing. Punishing my body through exercise will not bring me the joy I seek.

50

A Culture of Unity

I appeal to you, dear brothers and sisters, by the authority
of our Lord Jesus Christ, to live in harmony with each
other. Let there be no divisions in the church. Rather,
be of one mind, united in thought and purpose.

1 CORINTHIANS 1:10

Just hearing the word "politics" makes many of us cringe, balk, or disengage. Most would agree that, over the past few years, we have moved away from a peaceful understanding of differing political viewpoints to a reactionary environment that feels abrasive and even intimidating. Of course, opinions in and of themselves are not wrong. What feels tiresome and difficult is the tendency many of us have to try to convert others to our side instead of seeking to understand them. This leaves the topic of politics feeling like a modern-day minefield, one we may not be trained to navigate. Today's verse, 1 Corinthians 1:10, hands us a metaphorical map to navigating this minefield, identifying the mines and asking us to work together to deactivate them. It advocates that we work alongside our Christian brothers and sisters, whether or not we agree with them politically. Avoidance will not deactivate these mines; only working toward unity will.

While divisions of any kind, in the church and out, can be detrimental to relationships, the call to unity is especially important if you have a personal relationship with Christ. Harmony, also known as unity or peace, is of even greater significance for Christians because it is motivated by Jesus's calling for us to love others. A love for one another, drawn first from Christ's unending love for us, is enough to break ground with those who disagree. Loving one another is Jesus's second greatest commandment behind loving God (Matthew 22:36–40) and produces a harmony that unites even the most divided "in thought and purpose" (1 Corinthians 1:10).

Only when we are motivated by love can we work alongside one another to deactivate these political landmines. When we invest in growing our relationship with God through prayer, we develop the attitude and works of the Holy Spirit, of which love, patience, and perseverance are all a part (Galatians 5:22–23). In a divisive conversation about politics or current events, we can bring the temperature down by going to God in prayer. A prayer as simple as "help me seek unity" can realign us to the work of love. Creating a culture of unity, seeing others first and foremost as those created in God's image, will be complex and difficult. But the reward is richer and deeper community. The Holy Spirit will guide us, not divide us.

EMBRACING WHOLENESS

My opinions are not more important than my relationships. With the help of the Holy Spirit, I can create a culture of unity around me.

51

Confidence in Him

For the LORD will be your confidence and
will keep your foot from a snare.
PROVERBS 3:26 CSB

Building your confidence is a journey, and that's okay. Even as you grow in the knowledge of what it means to be made in God's image, there will be times when you doubt yourself or succumb to the messages all around you: messages that tell you to change, to improve, and to work harder to be worthy of love. You may doubt your abilities, your looks, or your decisions. When you get into this spiral of self-doubt and discouragement, how can you pull yourself out by leaning on the confidence of God? The process feels very abstract.

So how do you find your confidence in God when you feel so insecure? Being confident in God means depending on Him and trusting that He has a great plan for your life. It means choosing to trust God in the everyday moments, knowing His ways are greater than anything you could muster up on your own. Confidence in Him echoes Hebrews 13:6 (NIV), which says, "So we say with confidence, 'The Lord is my helper; I will not be afraid. What can mere mortals do to me?'"

Praying more and building your trust in God may not immediately dissipate your insecurities, your self-consciousness, or your fears. But what it can do is shift your focus from where you feel you may be lacking. When we feel self-conscious, we often hyper fixate on ourselves and on what we do not have. Switching our focus to the security and safety of our relationship with God builds a new kind of confidence, one that is eternal, an assurance of God's always abiding presence. This confidence is not rooted in anything we can do and is not temporary like our looks or our actions. Any confident moments we have in ourselves—based on appearance, personality, or accomplishments—originated with God anyway, the one who created us to flourish.

Building your confidence in God looks like reminding yourself of the truth of who He says you are: valuable (Job 33:4), set free (Psalm 27:1), beloved (Jeremiah 31:3), bold (2 Corinthians 3:12), and heard (1 Peter 3:13). By identifying ways in which your confidence is often shaken and counteracting those lies with the truth of Scripture, your confidence will grow. When you face moments of doubt or self-deprecation, remember that God is always with you. He will be your confidence when you feel you don't have any (1 John 3:20–21).

EMBRACING WHOLENESS

I put my confidence and my hope in God today, knowing He will sustain me.

Switching our focus
to the security
and safety of our
relationship with
God builds a new
kind of confidence.

52

For When You Doubt the Process

Do not fear, for I am with you; do not be afraid, for I am your God. I will strengthen you; I will help you; I will hold on to you with my righteous right hand.

ISAIAH 41:10 CSB

Working on your relationship with your body is hard—partially because healing is hard, and partially because you can never separate yourself from the work, as your body is always there. It's not like you can put your body away for a day or two and revisit it when you feel a little calmer or more at peace. The process of rebuilding your confidence requires dissecting layers of negativity that have accumulated over the years—layers of comparison, shame, and doubt. Just as physical wounds require time and attention to heal, our emotional wounds surrounding our body deserve the same care. Sometimes this can feel frustrating or exhausting. Some days you just feel tired, when you wonder if all this work is really worth it. But the truth is, you'll only be worse off if you never go through the hard to the healing that's waiting for you on the other side. Don't give up because the healing is hard.

Embracing your worth as God's creation will be a nonlinear journey. There will be amazing days with victorious steps forward. And there will also be times of difficult setbacks. Yet, every bit of momentum, every time you become aware of your inner critic, every change you make in the way you talk about your body, and every thought pattern you shift are a testament to your courage and determination to heal and rebuild your confidence. The process is full of ups and downs, but it is worth it.

As you heal, remember that your body is not your enemy but your ally. It's not a source of shame but a source of strength. It's not a deterrent to progress but the key to progress itself. It's not an accident but a purposeful creation of God. Even when you doubt the process, your Creator is there to reassure you, strengthen you, and guide you. He calls you fearfully and wonderfully made (Psalm 139:14).

EMBRACING WHOLENESS

I affirm that healing my relationship with my body is a journey worth pursuing. I choose to celebrate the small victories and extend grace to myself on the difficult days.

53

The Bleeding Woman

"Daughter," he said to her, "your faith has saved you. Go in peace."

LUKE 8:48 CSB

Imagine having your period for twelve years. The cramps, the headaches, the exhaustion, the emotional ups and downs, the bleeding. This is what the woman in Luke 8 was dealing with (for the complete narrative, see Matthew 9:20–22; Mark 5:25–34; Luke 8:43–48). She was no doubt exhausted, desperate for bodily healing, but resigned to the fact that her circumstances would not change. The text even says she'd "spent all she had on doctors and yet could not be healed by any" (Luke 8:43 CSB). She was dejected and alone, and she probably felt like her body was completely out of her control . . . but she had faith.

Because she was bleeding, this woman would have been considered unclean according to Jewish law. This meant she was not only barred from the temple but was labeled an outcast from society. Her body prohibited her from community and relationships. It would have taken tremendous determination and courage for her to join a crowd in the first place, for fear that someone would recognize her, and she would be punished for getting too close to others. In Jewish law, if she touched even one person, that person was also considered unclean. The stakes were high. Yet she not only joined the crowd by faith, but reached out and touched Jesus's garment. Her faith was so strong that she believed just a touch could heal her. When Jesus realized what had happened, He didn't scold her for breaking the law or approaching Him in her so-called unclean state, as she may have expected. Instead, Jesus healed her. He saw how great her faith was, and she was made whole once again.

No matter what your body is going through, no matter how hard you feel the healing journey is, keep the faith. In Matthew 17, Jesus says: "For truly I tell you, if you have faith the size of a mustard seed, you will tell this mountain, 'Move from here to there,' and it will move. Nothing will be impossible for you" (v. 20 CSB). The bleeding woman had tried everything, exhausting all her resources in the process, and yet she kept her faith. Jesus is the Healer of the broken, the Mender of the wounded, and the Restorer of the outcast. Jesus can rebuild your relationship with your body, even if this feels like an impossible ask. Nothing is impossible for Him.

EMBRACING WHOLENESS

Even when I feel as if I have nothing left, I can reach out to Jesus in faith. He will always be there, ready to listen and restore.

54

Beyond Body Beauty

Don't be concerned about the outward beauty of fancy
hairstyles, expensive jewelry, or beautiful clothes. You
should clothe yourselves instead with the beauty that
comes from within, the unfading beauty of a gentle
and quiet spirit, which is so precious to God.

1 PETER 3:3–4

A majority focus of body positivity is related to healing our relationship with our physical body, learning to respect, cherish,
and even love the body we have. This is good, essential healing. Our
relationship to our outward appearance is important, and yet we also
acknowledge that our true beauty—our inherent worth—comes
from within. But accepting that inner beauty comes from within,
as described in 1 Peter 3:4, is a weighty task. For many of us within
the Christian subculture, the concept of inner beauty may have been
an argument used to dismiss our complicated feelings about our
appearance or leveraged as a Bible Band-Aid to cover up our real
self-esteem issues. Maybe the idea of a gentle and quiet spirit feels
like a call to shut down our real selves in order to fit into a beauty
ideal. This couldn't be further from the truth.

True beauty doesn't look like a woman who subdues her personality, dismisses her passions, and shelves her dreams to fade into the
background. This is not God's heart for us. Instead, the wisdom
from today's passage about "the unfading beauty of a gentle and
quiet spirit" emphasizes that God is honored when your spirit, the

essence of who you are, is at rest in Him. When you have a deep relationship with the Lord, you reflect the fruit of the Spirit, of which gentleness is a part (Galatians 5:22–23). Your true, deep, inward beauty shines forth because your confidence comes from God, not from your body. This is why Peter, the author of this book, warns against hairstyles, jewelry, and clothes. He's warning us against the temptation to use external things to validate and secure our identity as a beautiful person.

Grounding our identity in an unshakable inner beauty starts with rejecting negative self-talk and replacing it with a confidence in God alone (see Hebrews 13:6). God's view of beauty differs drastically from the world's standards. He cherishes the qualities that often go unnoticed by human eyes: kindness, compassion, love, and a heart surrendered to Him. These attributes establish the base of a gentle and quiet spirit, the source of our unfading beauty that goes far beyond our physical body. We reflect the image of God as we grow closer to Him and display His goodness, His joy, and the beauty of a relationship with Him.

EMBRACING WHOLENESS

Even while I heal my relationship with my body, I acknowledge that my greatest beauty lies within.

55

Christ, the Image of God

He is the image of the invisible God, the
firstborn over all creation.

COLOSSIANS 1:15 CSB

No one better reflects the image of God than Jesus Christ Himself. Yes, Jesus is God, but He also mirrored God in His humanity when He came to earth as a baby. He reflected God in the same way we reflect the image of God. Second Corinthians 4:6 describes how we can see the glory of God through the Person of Jesus (see also Hebrews 1:3). Jesus Himself emphasizes His image-bearer relationship to His disciples in John 14:8–9. This passage states: "'Lord,' said Philip, 'show us the Father, and that's enough for us.' Jesus said to him, 'Have I been among you all this time and you do not know me, Philip? The one who has seen me has seen the Father. How can you say, "Show us the Father"?'"

Jesus is made in God's image and is also God Himself. This is only one element of the mystery of the Trinity. Remember that Genesis 1:26 states, "Let us make mankind in *our* image, in *our* likeness" (emphasis mine). This could be a reference to the three Persons of the Trinity: Father, Son, and Holy Spirit. Jesus was there in the garden of Eden when humanity was created in God's image. And at the same time, He was also created in God's image. When Jesus came down to earth, He was fully God and fully man (see Philippians 2:6–8). While this information is enough to make our head spin, it's also an opportunity to remind us that Jesus also lived here on earth, in a body, as an image bearer of God. The way we live out being made in the image of God is very different from Jesus. He was a perfect human who did not sin, and yet we have this imago Dei status in common with Christ. How special!

Through Jesus Christ and His sacrifice on the cross, we can come into a relationship with God and know Him. It is through Jesus that we can relate to God as His image bearers, reflecting His character and His goodness. Today, as we wrestle with what it means for Christ to be made in God's image while also being a member of the Trinity, may we rest in the amazing truth that we reflect God's image here on earth, just as Jesus did.

EMBRACING WHOLENESS

I may not fully understand the Trinity—God the Father, Jesus the Son, and the Holy Spirit—but even in the midst of my questions, I choose to worship my God, who made me in His image and who delights in me.

56

Mental Health Matters

Come to me, all you who are weary and
burdened, and I will give you rest.

MATTHEW 11:28 NIV

The importance of mental health is a big cultural conversation today—and for good reason. As the World Health Organization defines it, "Mental health is a state of mental well-being that enables people to cope with the stresses of life, realize their abilities, learn well and work well, and contribute to their community. It is an integral component of health and well-being that underpins our individual and collective abilities to make decisions, build relationships and shape the world we live in."[29] Not only is taking care of our own mental health important, but engaging in the cultural conversation around mental health encourages honesty, community, and love in both the joyous seasons and the hard ones. Only good things can come from increased awareness of what those around us might be going through.

Mr. Rogers once said, "Anything that's human is mentionable, and anything that is mentionable can be more manageable. When we can talk about our feelings, they become less overwhelming, less upsetting, and less scary."[30] So many of us are susceptible to hard days; seasons where we feel depressed or anxious; or dark nights, where we wonder if we even matter. Because we are afraid of judgment from others or feel shame from within, we can be tempted to keep big, scary feelings inside. But the lies that tell you that you are not important, that others won't understand, that this is a problem only you struggle with are just that—lies. When we recognize them as such and step out bravely, trusting others to take some of the weight of our big feelings off our shoulders, we can find relief, respite, and community. You'll find that when you are more open with your relationship with mental health, it also naturally encourages those around you to open up too.

EMBRACING WHOLENESS

My mental health matters. Today, I have the opportunity to be honest with God and with trusted friends about how I'm really doing.

57

Challenging Consumerism

Keep your lives free from the love of money and be
content with what you have, because God has said,
"Never will I leave you; never will I forsake you."

HEBREWS 13:5 NIV

Advertisements promise a new alarm clock that will make you a
morning person, a special journal that will help you find healing, and a big water bottle that will up your hydration game forever.
They tout something new and better that promises an easier, more
productive, more social media–worthy life. We are inundated with
these messages that we need more: something extra, something
great, something improved and enhanced. We see headlines in commercials or splashed across magazines, in ads on social media, and
in interviews with our favorite celebrities, all reinforcing our lack.
And suddenly we find ourselves stuck in a spiral of consumerism,
buying things because we want to feel better, to feel different. But
buying the next big thing will never heal us, free us, or soothe us
in the way we want it to. Sure, it may provide us with a temporary
dopamine rush, but that feeling is far too short-lived when we come
across the next sponsored post or pop-up ad. It just might be time
for us to break free.

When we get out of the constant cycle of consumerism, we may
see with clarity that we have power and opportunity to decide

exactly what we want. Freeing yourself from this cycle could be as simple as waiting two to three days between finding something you like and purchasing it. Or consider budgeting, or making a list of things you'd like to find at thrift stores, or deleting your account on a couple of online shopping websites. How you use the money God has entrusted to you is your choice, and these actions remind you of that.

Enjoying shopping is not a bad or sinful thing, but some of us are trapped in a cycle of consumerism we unknowingly fell into. When you recognize this pattern, you can take steps to make more mindful choices instead. Consumerism tells us our worth is found in what we acquire, but God tells us we are worthy just as we are.

EMBRACING WHOLENESS

I am significant not because of what I can buy, the way my home looks, the way I dress, or how stylish I am. My worth is found in God, and I reflect His image.

58

Happiness in Him

The one who understands a matter finds success, and
the one who trusts in the LORD will be happy.

PROVERBS 16:20 CSB

Many of us have envisioned a future for ourselves where we are brimming with confidence, never to struggle with body image again. But this future often hinges on changing or altering our body in often drastic ways, setting ourselves up in an alternate reality where a new and improved body boosts our happiness and garners compliments from those all around us. But obtaining your ideal body will not make you happy. Losing weight, toning your arms, smoothing your wrinkles—none of this will bring you lasting happiness, because these are all temporary fixes to address our surface problems.

Diet culture reinforces over and over again the lie that a new body will bring us happiness, constantly promoting new weight-loss plans, gym memberships, and groundbreaking diets. Social media influencers stare back at us with perfectly sculpted bodies, radiating a joy they might not even feel but seek to portray. So, we find ourselves seeking happiness and contentment in the reflection we see in the mirror, hoping that one day, we will attain that elusive perfect body. But as we resist diet culture and rebuild our relationship with our body, we look always to this truth: only a relationship with Jesus will bring us true, deep, lasting happiness in this life.

When we base our happiness solely in our physical appearance, we set ourselves up for disappointment. There will always be a new standard, a new diet, a new hurdle to our happiness. Conversely, a relationship with Jesus surpasses the elusive happiness standards of our earthly existence. As we pray, read His Word, and surround ourselves with His people, we experience a happiness that is not dependent on our looks, our circumstances, or our status. Instead, it's rooted in His promise that we are His children (Galatians 3:26), created in His image (Genesis 1:27) for a great purpose (Jeremiah 29:11). Not circumstantial or situational, this kind of happiness is lasting—and it looks a lot like joy, like freedom. So, we do not place our hopes for a happy life in our body, in our plans to change ourselves. Instead, we invest our time into a fruitful relationship with our Lord Jesus, who not only heals our view of self but also offers us incomparable happiness for this life and the next.

EMBRACING WHOLENESS

I will never find happiness in the pursuit of my ideal body. True happiness is found in Christ alone.

59

Weight Does Not Equal Worth

Are not five sparrows sold for two pennies? Yet not
one of them is forgotten by God. Indeed, the very
hairs of your head are all numbered. Don't be afraid;
you are worth more than many sparrows.

LUKE 12:6–7 NIV

As a society, we've placed a lot of value on a person's weight. One study found the following: "More than half of girls and one-third of boys as young as 6 to 8 feel their ideal body is thinner than their current body size."[31] This is heartbreaking. And while changing society's weight stigma will take time, it starts with us as individuals. We can break this stigma in our own hearts and positively influence those around us by remembering that God created us in His very image. This fact alone makes us worthy of love. A person's weight does not, and will not ever, determine their worth.

Our weight-obsessed culture would tell us that to be thin is to be a better person. As we see in television, movies, and social media, those who are thin are assumed to be more put together, more disciplined, more worthy of our admiration. It's easy to dismiss such logic when it's presented this plainly. However, most of us unconsciously reflect the weight stigma we see around us, judging the number on the scale and the reflection in the mirror and equating it with our importance. Luckily, God meets us even here with tender correction and grace, only ever reminding us of our immeasurable value.

As today's passage explains, God cares for all His creation, seeing it all as good and worthy of receiving His love and attention. Remember too that although God created the sparrows He tenderly nurtures, He didn't create them in His image as He created us. It's absurd to think that our Creator would judge us based on our weight, would give more thought to those of us who fit into a societal mold that prizes an acceptable weight. If the Lord of the universe looks at us and sees our weight for what it is, an arbitrary number, why should we do any different?

EMBRACING WHOLENESS

My worth is not determined by my weight. I am fearfully and wonderfully made, cherished by my Creator. My value is eternal, rooted in His love for me.

60

An Eternal Mindset

For we do not have an enduring city here; instead,
we seek the one to come. Therefore, through him let
us continually offer up to God a sacrifice of praise,
that is, the fruit of lips that confess his name.

HEBREWS 13:14–15 CSB

Famines, hurricanes, disease, poverty, hunger. Our world is broken and full of problems. And we can't fix it. But we weren't meant to. Because, if you are a follower of Christ, this world is not your home. We live here for, at most, eighty to ninety years, experiencing hardship and stress right alongside joys and celebration. We certainly try our best to create a temporary home that is safe, cozy, and loving. This is not a bad thing! But our true home is in heaven, as today's passage explains. The good things we have here—the homes we create, the relationships that thrive—are only a glimpse of the stunning goodness to come when we live in eternity with God.

The idea that this earth is only our temporary home could freak out those of us who are planners. But when we shift our view to this eternal perspective, we may find our day-to-day stressors feel just a bit lighter. So, if you are a planner, plan on your relationship with God sealing your beautiful forever with Him. In light of eternity in heaven, many burdens feel easier to bear in the here and now.

Colossians 3:1 (CSB) states: "So if you have been raised with Christ, seek the things above, where Christ is, seated at the right hand of God." To set our minds on things above doesn't mean we blatantly ignore the problems of our world and the needs of those around us. On the contrary, if we follow Jesus, serving others is an important part of the faith walk (see Matthew 20:26–28). To adopt a heavenly mindset is to allow the temporary problems of this world to be just that—temporary. By praying, reading Scripture, and growing in our relationship with God, we will often find that an eternal perspective is a natural overflow of a deeper relationship with Him. When we set our mind on things above, we find that our mind is more aligned with the mind of Christ—a mind of peace, love, and purity.

EMBRACING WHOLENESS

I set my eyes on heaven today, knowing eternity will be more glorious than I can imagine.

61

Beauty Standards

Charm is deceptive, and beauty is fleeting; but a
woman who fears the LORD is to be praised.

PROVERBS 31:30 NIV

As we scroll through social media or flip through channels trying to find something to watch, we're bombarded with shockingly beautiful people. From selfies, to sponsored ads, to special guests on your favorite television show, we are overrun with images of people who look practically perfect. This one might have amazing style, while the next person has clear, smooth skin, while another has the coveted hourglass figure. But these people, these images, are incredibly curated. They are crafted to reinforce a standard of beauty, one that we aren't measuring up to—and we weren't created to.

We set up as the standard people whose image is unattainable for most of us, thus creating impossible criteria for ourselves. In this way, we define what we, as a culture, see as valuable or attractive. Then we shame ourselves for not being able to attain it. To compare our bodies to those we see on television, on red carpets, and on social media is to set ourselves up for disappointment. Most celebrities who fit this standard of beauty have disposable income to spend on private chefs, makeup artists, trainers, and stylists. Actress Blake Lively is even quoted as saying, "It's so important for young people not to compare themselves with what they see online. . . . It's our job as actors and/or models to be in shape. We have access to gyms and trainers and healthy food. And then on top of that, 99.9 percent of the time the images are Photoshopped."[32]

Recognizing and resisting the beauty standards of the day is difficult, but it is not impossible. It begins with a foundational decision to anchor our heart in the truths of Scripture, not in the changing standards of the world. As today's passage reminds us, our relationship with God will outlast any charm or beauty we gain in this life. How freeing! We are not created in the image of an ever-changing and often unattainable beauty standard, but in the image of a loving God who knew exactly what our body would look like and how we would use it to glorify Him.

EMBRACING WHOLENESS

Beauty standards were created to make me feel less than. God says I am always enough in Him.

62

The Appearance of Jesus

My servant grew up in the LORD's presence like a tender green shoot, like a root in dry ground. There was nothing beautiful or majestic about his appearance, nothing to attract us to him.

ISAIAH 53:2

Isaiah 53 prophesies the coming of a Messiah who will carry our sorrows, be wounded for our transgressions, and atone for our sin. This Messiah is Jesus Christ, our Lord. As Isaiah 53 describes Jesus, the prophet Isaiah writes, "there was nothing beautiful or majestic about his appearance, nothing to attract us to him" (v. 2). In other words, Jesus wasn't particularly good-looking, He wouldn't have stood out from the crowd. The Message paraphrases verse 2 this way: "There was nothing attractive about him, nothing to cause us to take a second look." As those caught up in a culture that uses our good looks as social currency, this verse reminds us of two important truths: good looks do not determine our worth, and our attractiveness is not a concern to our God.

Numerous studies show that beautiful people are believed to be more popular and more highly respected than less attractive people. This physical-attractiveness stereotype is also called "what is beautiful is good."[33] When Jesus came down to earth, born as a human, God could have easily made Him the most beautiful person we've ever seen. He could have formed Him to fit the highest beauty standards of the day, to catch people's eye every time He was out in public. Perhaps this would have made His message more popular to

> **Jesus didn't come to dazzle us but to transform us.**

some, those looking for a public figure who dazzles and shines. But Jesus didn't come to dazzle us but to transform us. He didn't come to grab our attention for a minute but to transform our hearts for a lifetime.

Remembering that Jesus, the most important man to ever live, was not concerned with appearance gives us the freedom to readjust our scale for determining our worth. Even if the world says, "What it beautiful is good," Scripture says, "Then God looked over all he had made, and he saw that it was very good!" (Genesis 1:31). Your worth is not, and has never been, determined by the worldly standards of attractiveness. God said you were good from the start because you were made in His image. "The LORD doesn't see things the way you see them. People judge by outward appearance, but the LORD looks at the heart" (1 Samuel 16:7).

EMBRACING WHOLENESS

The way I look is the least important thing about me. God created me and called me "very good" (Genesis 1:31).

63

Healing from Hurtful Words

The words of the reckless pierce like swords, but
the tongue of the wise brings healing.

PROVERBS 12:18 NIV

The words of others are dangerously powerful. So powerful in fact that most of us carry wounds from the past: remarks someone made out of anger, envy, or hurt that we carry with us day after day. Maybe a friend made an offhanded comment about your personality, a bully mocked something about your appearance, or a family member criticized the way you live in the heat of an argument. Those words cut deep. Even if it was years ago, the wound is still scabbed, not healed. And in moments of self-doubt or when someone says something even remotely similar, you feel the wound open again.

We don't have remedies to heal from this "unwholesome talk" on our own because deep down, we fear that it might be true. But when we bring these wounds to the great Physician, we can receive healing for today and strength for tomorrow. In Him, we are reminded of who we are, and we are healed from hurtful lies. The great Physician not only treats our wounds; He gives us the remedy for rejecting these lies in the future. As you think on the way others' words have wounded you in the past, know that God is ready and able to heal you. Jeremiah 17:14 (NIV) says: "Heal me, LORD, and

I will be healed; save me and I will be saved, for you are the one I praise." We can come to Him in prayer, giving our hurts over to Him.

As we remember ways in which others spoke that did not build us up, we can find strength in the way God affirms us. He says in Christ, you are a friend of God (James 2:23), you are free from condemnation (Romans 8:1–2), you are a citizen of heaven (Philippians 3:20), you are empowered by the very strength of Christ (Philippians 4:13). You have the ability to reject the lies spoken about you. When we bring these lies to Christ, we are reminded that we are made in the very image of God. We are told we are cherished, we are free, and we are being made more like Christ every day (2 Corinthians 4:16).

EMBRACING WHOLENESS

Today I walk in the truth of who God says I am. I step toward healing from wounds others have caused me with harsh and hurtful words, knowing the truest thing about me is that I am in Christ.

64

Self-Acceptance

For we are God's masterpiece. He has created us anew in Christ
Jesus, so we can do the good things he planned for us long ago.

EPHESIANS 2:10

God didn't just create your body, your physical form, in His
image; He also lovingly crafted your personality, who you
are. Your quick wit, your goofy side, your intellectual nature, your
extroversion or introversion—you reflect the character of God. And
it is a gift to others when you live out your unique attributes. For
many of us, however, self-acceptance is a difficult road. It is Christ
who redeems us and makes us whole, so apart from Him, we focus
on our failings, areas of our hearts and our lives that are in desperate need of change and growth. While we know we are sinners in
need of His grace, we also know we are loved by Christ as we are
right now. He transforms us when we are in a relationship with
Him. Second Corinthians 5:17 (csb) puts it this way: "Therefore,
if anyone is in Christ, he is a new creation; the old has passed away,
and see, the new has come!"

Living with Christ at the center of each day amplifies our God-
given personality while simultaneously helping us come to terms
with all aspects of ourselves. This is what self-acceptance is all about,
learning to view every part of ourselves without conditions or judgment, seeing ourselves honestly but without condemnation, just as
Christ sees us. Author David Benner writes in his book *The Gift of
Being Yourself*: "Genuine self-knowledge begins by looking at God

and noticing how God is looking at us." He wrote later: "Paradoxically, as we become more and more like Christ, we become more uniquely our own true self."[34] So we embrace ourselves as a unique creation of God, acknowledging both our strengths and weaknesses, working on becoming at peace with ourselves. And as we draw closer to Him by praying, reading the Word, and getting into Christian community, we see just how we each uniquely reflect the image of God. Through self-acceptance, we can not only see our personalities as a gift from God, we can also cultivate deeper relationships with others, seeing that we are all exceptional reflections of an immeasurably good Lord.

EMBRACING WHOLENESS

My worth is not defined by worldly standards but rather by the immeasurable value I have in Christ. It is a gift to others when I embrace myself for all that I am.

65

Sabbath

Then he said to them, "The Sabbath was made
for man, not man for the Sabbath."

MARK 2:27 NIV

We are exhausted and overstimulated. We feel like we need a long nap, a few hours to numb out in front of the television, or a piping hot bath. But even when we make time for some self-care, we often don't feel as rejuvenated as we envisioned. That's because what we really need is the rest of God. Enter Sabbath.

Sabbath, a weekly rhythm of rest and worship, was created by God to draw us back to Him. It was meant to give us true, reenergizing rest, realigning our priorities and calming that hustle in our heart. The great news is, we can claim this day of rest as a promise from Jesus Himself, marking it as a time set aside to recalibrate and reorient our hearts in Him. As author Mark Buchanan explains:

> Without rest, we miss the rest of God: the rest he invites us to enter more fully so that we might know him more deeply. . . . Sabbath is both a day and an attitude to nurture such stillness. It is both time on a calendar and a disposition of the heart. It is a day we enter, but just as much a way we see. Sabbath imparts the rest of God—actual physical, mental, spiritual rest, but also the rest of God— the things of God's nature and presence we miss in our busyness.[35]

This may sound like a great idea, but it could feel unattainable. Maybe you feel too busy, or you just aren't sure what the rest of God looks like practically for your life. So start small. A Sabbath isn't meant to turn into some legalistic set of rules, forcing you to rest because you feel like you're supposed to. It can be any day, any period of time. To enjoy Sabbath rest is to do things that you enjoy, that bring you back to God, that feel restful. This could mean you spend a day each week sleeping in, spending extra time reading your Bible, and going on a long walk with friends. It could look like cooking an elaborate meal with your family and getting away from the house to journal and pray, taking twenty-four hours off dishes and laundry. There is no wrong way to rest, God just wants you to come to Him. Take time this week to "be still, and know" (Psalm 46:10).

EMBRACING WHOLENESS

I am not too busy to seek the rest of God. In Him, I can find renewal and spiritual nourishment in the midst of life.

66

Sizes

A tranquil heart is life to the body, but
jealousy is rottenness to the bones.

PROVERBS 14:30 CSB

It's all too easy to fall into the trap of comparison where we evaluate our own worth against the appearance of others. Ads, social media, movies, and television lay this trap out for us, telling us that only one type of body size is beautiful, acceptable, and healthy. We take this in, consciously or unconsciously, and use this problematic standard to compare ourselves to our friends, neighbors, and family. In the process, we try to decide if we are close enough to the standard to be beautiful. This is a problem in and of itself, but we also use this standard to reassure ourselves of our standing in society. We allow jealousy and judgment to secure us in this trap, as we think hurtful untruths we would never say out loud like, *At least I'm not as big as her*, or, *She is so skinny, so she must be so happy*, or, *She must be unhealthy; I'm doing better than her*. Although it's difficult, we have to recognize and address this phobia against bodies of different sizes so we can free ourselves from the comparison trap, stepping into healing our relationship with our own bodies.

Our outward appearance will never tell the full story of our health: mental, emotional, and physical. Yet we have gotten so used to using it as our main measuring stick to determine worth and goodness. So today, whether you are much bigger, much smaller, or around the same size as those in your immediate circle, may you liberate yourself from the jealousy and judgment and instead embrace your size as an intentional part of who you are.

To develop a "tranquil heart" (Proverbs 14:30 CSB), as today's verse references, we develop eyes to see the pitfalls our size-obsessed culture has designed for us. When you catch yourself judging someone based on their weight, ask yourself: Is this person created in the image of God? What do I seek to accomplish by judging their weight against my own? How else can I fill this need to judge and compare? This awareness of our own faulty thinking not only brings clarity in our connection with our body but also can draw us to God in prayer. Through our relationship with Him, lies are replaced with truth and judgment is replaced with joy. God created you in His image, and He knew what size you would be.

EMBRACING WHOLENESS

I can acknowledge and resist jealousy and comparison today, knowing that God created me and blessed me as I am.

67

What Communion Means

For I pass on to you what I received from the Lord himself. On the night when he was betrayed, the Lord Jesus took some bread and gave thanks to God for it. Then he broke it in pieces and said, "This is my body, which is given for you. Do this in remembrance of me." In the same way, he took the cup of wine after supper, saying, "This cup is the new covenant between God and his people—an agreement confirmed with my blood. Do this in remembrance of me as often as you drink it." For every time you eat this bread and drink this cup, you are announcing the Lord's death until he comes again.

1 CORINTHIANS 11:23–26

Jesus lived on earth in a physical body, just like ours. Yet, He forfeited this body and His life, subjecting Himself to great suffering on our behalf so we could have a relationship with God. We honor this sacrifice of body, of blood, of life through communion. If you have attended church for any length of time, you have likely seen people take communion or have taken it yourself. It involves eating a small piece of bread or cracker and drinking a sip of grape juice or wine. When we participate in this sacred ritual of communion, we are reminded of the incredible cost that the Lord paid for us—one that involved His very body. His physical body was a sacrifice for our redemption. So, we honor Christ when we live as fully embodied people, ones who have been redeemed.

Before He was betrayed and surrendered to the authorities, Jesus shared this meal with His dearest companions, His disciples, breaking the bread and pouring the wine. At that time, they couldn't fully comprehend the weight of His words, unaware that He would soon be crucified for their sins. Today, with the full story revealed, when we participate in communion, we honor His sacrifice—a sacrifice that included His earthly body, a body formed in Mary's womb years earlier and bearing the imago Dei.

When we look to Christ's sacrifice for us on the cross and acknowledge the forgiveness and redemption that flow from His broken body by taking communion, we remember that He gave all of Himself for all of us. He died so that you might have life (1 Thessalonians 5:10), and that abundant life includes freedom from body shame. Jesus gave His body for you.

EMBRACING WHOLENESS

Jesus gave all of Himself for me, and I honor Him with my body and pursuit of self-love today.

When we participate in the sacred ritual of communion, we are reminded of the incredible cost that the Lord paid for us—one that involved His very body.

68

You Are Worthy Now

But God demonstrates his own love for us in this:
While we were still sinners, Christ died for us.

ROMANS 5:8 NIV

When we are entrenched in comparison, self-doubt, and the diet culture, we lose faith in our intrinsic worth and value. We look inward and only find lack, forgetting our worthiness as those created in God's image. And when we are in that place, our culture will only always reinforce the idea that we need to do something new, change drastically, or revamp our whole life to be accepted, to be lovable. It will always leave us striving, depleted, and exhausted. While it's true that we are all sinners in need of grace, we don't need to muster up enough energy or grit to make ourselves lovable. We are worthy of God's great love and acceptance now. We are worth loving, just as we are.

Today's verse explains that God loved us *while* we were still sinners. This means that even prior to Christ's dying on the cross for our sins, prior to us entering a relationship with Him, God loved us. We were created out of that love, loved even before we were called by Christ our Savior. Therefore, nothing we do or don't do can change our worthiness in God's eyes or the immeasurable, unfathomable love He has for us. Lamentations 3 and Psalm 63 describe God's love as faithful, meaning it is our constant companion. As you process through your multifaceted relationship with your body, God's calming and steady love will be by your side. No change to your weight, your skincare routine, or your eating habits can affect your worth in the eyes of the Lord.

In a world that often promotes comparison and perfectionism, we remember that God's love for us is unconditional. We don't have to earn it; we simply receive it. It's a love that surpasses our perceived flaws, our failures, and even our insecurities. It's a love that says, "You are loved and worthy of love." First John 4:8 says that God is love, and this love is right by your side, every day. You are worthy of this love now.

EMBRACING WHOLENESS

I am enough just as I am today. As I work on my relationship with my body, I commit to seeing myself as lovable and worthy of love. In His eyes, I am valued, cherished, and loved beyond measure.

69

On Trusting God

Trust in the LORD with all your heart, and do
not rely on your own understanding.

PROVERBS 3:5 CSB

Take a moment and think of someone you trust completely—maybe it's a friend, a partner, or a family member. How do you feel when you are with that person? Safe, content, maybe even at home. To trust someone is to rely upon them, believing that they have your best interest at heart and will care for you because they value who you are. When you trust someone, you know they will stick by your side through the storms of life because, ultimately, they love you. Trust and love are intertwined, working together to create peace in a relationship. God is more trustworthy than even your closest confidant. He is all-knowing and all-powerful, capable of guiding and supporting you through any challenge life throws at you. You can trust God with your heart, with your story, and with your life because He is goodness, faithfulness, and love personified.

Psalm 9 says, "The LORD is a refuge for the persecuted, a refuge in times of trouble. Those who know your name trust in you because you have not abandoned those who seek you, LORD" (vv. 9–10 CSB). We grow trust in our relationships through time, and the same is true with God. If you aren't spending time with the Lord in prayer and reading His Word, it won't be easy to trust Him to carry your burdens, hear your prayers, and guide your life. We can't trust someone we don't know. But as you build a relationship with the One who made you in His image, you'll learn through personal experience just how trustworthy God is.

Through each prayer, each moment of comfort during a hard time, each encouragement found in Scripture just when you need it, you'll find it easier to give more and more of yourself over to God. In trust, we surrender ourselves to Him because we know that we are safe, and we are loved by Him.

EMBRACING WHOLENESS

I speak the words of Psalm 28:7 (CSB) over my life today: "The Lord is my strength and my shield; my heart trusts in him, and I am helped. Therefore my heart celebrates, and I give thanks to him with my song."

70

The Power of Words

The soothing tongue is a tree of life, but a
perverse tongue crushes the spirit.

PROVERBS 15:4 NIV

"They look like they've really let themselves go."
"Wow, I could never eat that big of a portion!"
"Ugh, I look so fat in this outfit."

We're all guilty of expressing this type of degrading remark at one time or another—about our body, about someone else's appearance, or about food and weight. While these comments often seem harmless, perhaps even used to bond with someone else or to fit in, we know deep down that they are anything but easily dismissed, casual comments. As we learn more about the complexity of our relationship with our body, we naturally become more mindful of how the words we speak about appearance and bodies affect others. You never know where someone else is on their journey with their body. These remarks can set others back in deep and upsetting ways, cutting to a person's core, even if the comment was not spoken about them. They may affirm insecurities those we love have never spoken aloud about their body or their relationship with food. This is because these comments are all rooted in comparison and self-esteem issues, causing self-reflection to listeners that can be hurtful to their healing.

Our words carry immense power. We must be cautious about how we speak, not only about ourselves, but about others as it relates to our body. When we criticize openly, we might inadvertently perpetuate a culture of self-doubt and discontent in those around us. Our speech can either build others up or tear them down, impacting how they perceive their own body and self-worth. As we work toward healing our relationship with our body, reorienting ourselves to the beauty of being made in God's image, we want to speak kindly over our own body and to those around us. Every one of us is on a different journey with our body, and we honor this journey when we use words that give life. Psalm 141:3 (NIV) says: "Set a guard over my mouth, LORD; keep watch over the door of my lips." With the help of our Lord, we can become more aware of ways in which we speak negatively about the image of God each of us carries in bodily form.

EMBRACING WHOLENESS

Making comments about bodies, food, and appearance can be harmful to those around me. Instead, I can speak life into each person's experience with their body as I learn to trust my own.

71

Excusing Away Our Appearance

So don't throw away your confidence, which has a great reward.

HEBREWS 10:35 csb

D o you ever feel like you have to make excuses for your appearance? It could be as obvious as "Sorry, I have a cold, so I look kinda gross," or "I really need to go shopping; I am showing up looking rough," or even "Just a heads up, I decided not to wear makeup today!" Or something more nuanced like, "My acne has been flaring up lately; it's so noticeable," or "I haven't been sleeping well, so my under-eye bags are pretty bad." It's almost a natural compulsion to make excuses for how we present ourselves. No matter how obvious our remarks are, they are all born of an insecurity that tells us we need to justify our appearance and apologize for our body. But we don't owe anyone an explanation as to why we look a certain way, why our bodies change, or why our appearance may be different. We are allowed to exist without apology and show up as we are.

These excuses not only root us in self-doubt; they also always cause comparison with others. When we try to explain away our appearance, it naturally causes those around us to look inward and compare. If we are complaining about our weight, but they are heavier, how will this make them feel? If we say we look bad, but they secretly wish they looked like us, what will this do for their self-confidence? Excusing away our appearance may feel like a way to temporarily ease our own insecurities, but in reality, it will only cause more body shame for us as it creates division in our relationships.

We free ourselves from any pressure to excuse away our appearance by first noticing and addressing our urge to do so. Why do we think we need to bring attention to our comfy clothes when we show up at a friend's house? What makes us feel it's necessary to call out our no-makeup look or lack of what we deem as being "put together"? What would happen if we resisted the urge to degrade or speak unkindly to our own body and instead stood in the confidence that our body is good because God created it that way—so we can show up however we choose?

EMBRACING WHOLENESS

I don't need to excuse away my body and my appearance. I can stand confidently in who I am today.

72

Being a Safe Person

Do not take revenge or bear a grudge against members of your community, but love your neighbor as yourself; I am the Lord.

LEVITICUS 19:18 CSB

N o matter our personality type, our past, our relationship history, our community that surrounds us—we all desire healthy human connection that feels authentically safe. As we strive to love our neighbor more deeply, we can become this person for others, creating an environment around us that is kind and loving. Part of reflecting the image of God is reflecting the character of God, growing to look more like Him as our relationship with Him deepens. He is complex and interesting, and we reflect the different aspects of who He is in our own complexity. And, as we embrace our status as image bearers of God, we can work toward becoming a person others feel safe with.

Being a safe person is a radical act of loving your neighbor well.

Being a safe person is a radical act of loving your neighbor well (Mark 12:31). It means creating a supportive and trustworthy environment for others simply through your presence, promoting emotional and spiritual well-being as you reflect His image to those around you. A safe person is someone who is not judgmental, and who meets others with understanding and empathy. Others feel comfortable around you, even if they don't know you that well, because you are trustworthy. Just as we can bring our whole selves to God in prayer and are met with grace and forgiveness (see 2 Corinthians 12:9; Ephesians 1:7; Hebrews 4:16), a safe person does not condemn others for their mistakes or struggles but offers understanding, empathy, and support. They seek to strengthen and empower others, encouraging them to rely on God while offering assurance and hope during difficult times. A safe person maintains confidentiality when entrusted with someone's story, committing to pray for others before anything else. A safe person also allows for disagreements, for confession of sin, for big emotions and big struggles. A safe person is a person who welcomes it all, just as God does. They are all these things and more, demonstrating God's love through their actions and reactions.

If this sounds overwhelming, it's because we are not meant to muster up our own strength to become a trustworthy, loving, safe person. We can only learn to love our neighbor this way by leaning on God Himself. As we draw closer to Him and grow in our relationship with Him, we naturally start to exemplify the safety we have found in Him to others. We can pray for others even as we pray for our own hearts to be open, growing to be that safe person we all need.

EMBRACING WHOLENESS

I commit today to creating a safe and nurturing space where others can find understanding, support, and growth.

73

Not a Hindrance

For God did not call us to be impure, but to live a holy life.

1 THESSALONIANS 4:7 NIV

Purity culture is a term often used to describe a movement that purported to promote a biblical view of purity. While the beginnings of purity culture were likely well intended, teaching young men and women to "flee sexual immorality" (see 1 Thessalonians 4:3–6) and live a life of holiness (see 1 Peter 1:13–16), the message became warped along the way. There were sermons, books, and conversations that told us our bodies are a hindrance to others' holiness, and our very existence as women could make men sin. This is a lie. You were not created to tempt or to satisfy a man. Putting so much emphasis on our bodies can lead us to internalize this belief. Your body was created "very good" all on its own (Genesis 1:31), and your very existence in that body is not a problem or an issue, but a purposeful act of God.

You are not responsible for the way others react to your body. While we can create "stumbling blocks" for others (see Romans 14:13 NIV)—like encouraging them to participate in a sinful behavior with us or acting promiscuously—our very existence as embodied women does no such thing. Extreme modesty and body shame will not help others avoid sin; it will only trap us in self-hatred. Your body is not bad. God didn't suffer design flaws when He created you; and the responsibility for someone else's purity does not fall solely on your shoulders. Yes, we can make it easier for someone to sin, but each person is responsible for their own choices and their own relationship with God. Sin is a condition of the heart, and you are not accountable for another person's heart. We can balance the responsibility of presenting our own body with dignity while not taking on the responsibility of another person's thoughts or actions.

Shake the shame off! Your body is not a problem, a hindrance, or an irredeemable issue. You may hear messages that your body's very existence causes others to lust, to think impure thoughts, or to sin. But what does God say about your body? Your body reflects His image (Genesis 1:27), is fearfully and wonderfully made (Psalm 139:13–16), and is holy, a temple of the Lord (1 Corinthians 3:16–17). God crafted all of you with immeasurable love and care, your body included.

EMBRACING WHOLENESS

I release any shame I carry that my body is a hindrance for others in their relationship with God. My body is not a problem.

74

Mary Magdalene, the Healed

After this, Jesus traveled about from one town and village to another, proclaiming the good news of the kingdom of God. The Twelve were with him, and also some women who had been cured of evil spirits and diseases: Mary (called Magdalene) from whom seven demons had come out.

LUKE 8:1–2 NIV

Before Mary Magdalene traveled with Jesus, watching Him perform great miracles and listening to Him teach huge crowds; before she stood weeping at the foot of the cross where her Savior was crucified; before she went to the tomb of Jesus and saw that it was empty; she was a woman tortured by seven demons. Mary Magdalene had probably lived her days as an outcast—avoided and shamed. She had likely given up all hope for healing, accepting that this was who she was. But Jesus saw her, the core of who she was, and He loved her. The darkness within her seemed impenetrable, but she was destined for redemption and healing.

While the text doesn't specify exactly how these demons used her, we can infer from other stories in the Bible like this that Mary Magdalene was not in control of her body. She may not have even been aware of her surroundings, of herself, of her very life, before Jesus healed her. He saw her in her tortured state, in her possessed body, and He delivered her. He healed her—body, spirit, soul—and she went on to follow Jesus as one of His disciples. When Mary encountered Jesus, everything changed. His presence alone brought hope into her world, a world that had been devoid of that for so many years. With compassion in His eyes, Jesus cast out the demons, liberating her from her years of suffering. She became a new creation, no longer defined by her past but by her relationship with the Savior, her Healer.

Jesus has the power to redeem and heal every part of us. As we see in the life of Mary Magdalene, He has a great plan for our lives, one that will not be inhibited by our struggles. With the Healer by your side, you can restore your relationship with your body and have strength for whatever you face in this life. Mary's story reminds us that Jesus is the ultimate Deliverer. His power to free us has no limit.

EMBRACING WHOLENESS

Jesus is my Healer and my Deliverer; I can give my struggles to Him today.

75

In Your Feels

Don't worry about anything; instead, pray about
everything. Tell God what you need and thank him for
all he has done. Then you will experience God's peace,
which exceeds anything we can understand. His peace will
guard your hearts and minds as you live in Christ Jesus.

PHILIPPIANS 4:6–7

As humans, we have big emotions. We feel a vast spectrum of
feelings: sadness, anger, joy, surprise, fear. We hear a lot of
rhetoric in this day and age about how feelings aren't facts. While
this is true, this statement paints emotions in a negative light, reinforcing that feelings aren't to be trusted or understood. But to say
we should discount or look upon our feelings with suspicion means
we miss out on the helpful and healing power of our emotions. God
created the whole of our being in His image, including our emotions.

Scripture reveals the Source of our emotional life, describing God
with a whole range of emotions, from love (1 John 4:8, Jeremiah
31:3) and joy (Zephaniah 3:17; Isaiah 62:5) to jealousy (Exodus
20:5; Joshua 24:19) and grief (Genesis 6:6; Psalm 78:40). Jesus
is also emotional, particularly shown when He was here on earth
through the examples of Matthew 23:33 (where He showed righteous indignation), John 2:13–17 (where He expressed disgust),
John 11:35 (where He felt grief), and Mark 14:33 and Matthew
26:37–39 (where He was so distraught, He sweat blood). If God
the Father and Jesus the Son, who are both perfect and without

sin, feel emotions this deeply, certainly we are not only allowed but encouraged to do the same. Through their example, as well as the examples of countless people in Scripture who displayed great emotion, we can be reassured that our feelings are important and worthy of being felt!

Today's Scripture doesn't say, "Do not worry about anything because your feelings can't be trusted." It says, "Don't worry about anything; instead, pray about everything" (Philippians 4:6). We can bring our feelings, no matter how big or small, to God in prayer, asking Him to soothe us and show us what is right. Feelings may not be facts, but they do point to the state of our heart and are meant to be paid attention to. When we feel our feels and ask God to help us decode them, He promises to give us His peace, one that will not come and go like our changing emotions.

EMBRACING WHOLENESS

My feelings are valid, no matter what they are. I can feel them, while also bringing them to God in prayer, knowing I'll be met with His healing, peace, and strength.

76

Self-Care

For no one ever hates his own flesh but provides
and cares for it, just as Christ does for the church,
since we are members of his body.

EPHESIANS 5:29–30 csb

Social media portrays self-care as a night at home with a face mask, bubble bath, and new craft. Television shows and movies demonstrate self-care as choosing yourself, even at the expense of others, making sure your happiness is the ultimate goal. But self-care is so much more than a selfishness rooted in personal preferences or a shopping trip to distract you from your feelings. As authors of *The Whole Life: 52 Weeks of Biblical Self-Care*, Eliza Huie and Esther Smith explain: "We define biblical self-care as 'the practice of drawing on divinely given resources to steward our whole lives for personal enrichment, the good of others, and the glory of God.'"[36] This means God has given us the resources to practice self-care in a way that restores us, encourages others, and draws us closer to Him.

A Christian view of self-care rebuilds our relationship with God. It means we slow down, putting our worries and our nagging anxieties back into His hands. It reminds us that we can't do it all, and we weren't meant to. As today's passage explains, God implanted the mechanism of self-care into us, to provide and care for our own bodies. When we care for ourselves, we are better connected and prepared to serve other members of Christ's body, the church. So the difference here is that Christian self-care restores your soul by anchoring you in the Lord instead of temporarily easing your fears by ignoring them or hurting others in the process.

What does this kind of radical self-care look like in your own life? Making a mental or physical list of ways you feel refreshed and connected to God is a good start. Maybe this looks like taking a long nap, catching up on Bible reading, or going on a walk in the forest. Or maybe it is changing your morning playlist from pop jams to worship music, getting your mind fixed on Jesus as you sit in traffic. God isn't asking you to care for yourself perfectly, but He is honored when your care for yourself in ways that draw you back to Him and refresh your soul.

EMBRACING WHOLENESS

I reflect the image of God when I care for myself in ways that nourish me and enrich my relationship with God and with others.

A Christian view of
self-care reminds
us that we can't
do it all, and we
weren't meant to.

77

Body Boundaries

For the grace of God has appeared that offers salvation
to all people. It teaches us to say "No" to ungodliness
and worldly passions, and to live self-controlled,
upright and godly lives in this present age.

TITUS 2:11–12 NIV

For some of us, *boundaries* is a scary word. It sounds like confronta-
tion, like opposition, like limitation. But boundaries can actually
be freeing and clarifying, and they don't have to involve conflict at
all. Without any boundaries, we will become accessible to others
at all times. This will only leave us feeling burned-out, exhausted,
and overstimulated. And Jesus never asked us to live overworked,
hurried, and overburdened. He calls us to freedom (Galatians 5:1),
a freedom that can be found by setting healthy and maintainable
boundaries. Healthy boundaries help us care for not only our inner
selves, but for our bodies as well.

As today's verse explains, God's grace teaches us to say no when
needed. Setting boundaries is biblical. After all, God's heart is to use
boundaries to protect us from harm and to free us to fully enjoy the
goodness He has planned for us. From the very beginning, God set
the world in motion with boundaries—He set boundaries for day
and night (Genesis 1:3–4), for land and sea (Genesis 1:6), and for
us. He gave humans rule over creation (Genesis 1:29) and directed
them what to eat and what not to eat (Genesis 2:16–17). We can
create many different types of boundaries, from boundaries on

our time and our possessions, to emotional boundaries, physical boundaries, and spiritual boundaries. Specifically in relation to our bodies, this may mean setting a boundary like leaving the room when others talk weight loss, never engaging in a discussion of someone else's appearance, or asking others not to discuss dieting with you. Body boundaries mean speaking up when you feel uncomfortable, whether it's something as simple as asking for a high five instead of a hug from an acquaintance or discussing your physical boundaries with a romantic partner. Boundaries around our bodies reinforce for us that we are in control of our bodies, that our bodies are worthy of love and respect. We do not live at the whim and desires of others. God created our bodies in His image, and we can dictate how we want to be treated as an embodied person.

When we set boundaries for ourselves, we declare that our bodies are not at the mercy of every demand or temptation that comes our way. Instead, we choose to steward our bodies with intentionality, knowing that our bodies are good. As you become more aware of your body, take time today to ask yourself what boundaries you may need to set. Know that God will meet you there, ready to help you take this step in your body confidence journey.

EMBRACING WHOLENESS

I can confidently set boundaries that protect and honor the body God has given me.

78

A Hospitable Mindset

Work willingly at whatever you do, as though you were
working for the Lord rather than for people. Remember
that the Lord will give you an inheritance as your reward,
and that the Master you are serving is Christ.

COLOSSIANS 3:23–24

We hear the word *hospitality* thrown around a lot these days among Christians. Used for good reason, to encourage us to open our hearts and our homes to those close to us and to those we do not know as well, hospitality is frequently emphasized in the pages of Scripture (see Isaiah 58:7; Hebrews 13:2; 1 Peter 4:9). Hospitality is defined as "the friendly reception and treatment of guests or strangers."[37] But, for many of us, the idea of hospitality feels uncomfortable, overwhelming, or even a little bit shameful. Maybe you live in a small home that easily feels cramped, maybe you feel embarrassed about your secondhand decor, or maybe you just see your home as your sanctuary—a place for you to rest, not to open to the outside world. Whatever the reason, if the idea of hospitality makes you cringe, it's okay. It has never been about a perfect meal, an immaculate home, or a host that is always "on." No, a hospitable mindset simply asks us to care for others, extending friendship by welcoming them into our real life—laundry piles, burnt chicken nuggets, and all.

God has not asked us to be perfect but to be faithful. We can feel apprehensive about allowing others into our space, both emotionally and physically. But as those made in His image, we reflect the way He welcomed us into His arms (despite our shortcomings, our mess-ups, and our general weirdness) when we do the same for others. When we adopt a mindset of hospitality, one that looks for opportunities to encourage others and show them love, we reflect God Himself. As Rosaria Butterfield writes in *The Gospel Comes with a House Key*, "Let God use your home, apartment, dorm room, front yard, community gymnasium, or garden for the purpose of making strangers into neighbors and neighbors into family. Because that is the point—building the church and living like a family, the family of God."[38] No matter the size, state, or aesthetics of your home, may you know that offering a safe space to others will expand your heart, provide for others, and please the Lord.

EMBRACING WHOLENESS

By extending open arms and creating a welcoming space, I reflect the hospitality and friendship God has shown me.

79

Heart Change

Look, I am about to do something new; even now
it is coming. Do you not see it? Indeed, I will make
a way in the wilderness, rivers in the desert.

ISAIAH 43:19 CSB

We've all done it. It's New Year's Eve, and we decide the next year is when we'll finally get in shape. Maybe we throw out all the desserts in our house, get a membership at a new gym, or purchase that new diet plan or cookbook. We feel motivated and inspired, picturing our new body, the compliments pouring in, the willpower we will be lauded for.

And then it's February . . . and we shamefully pretend we never made that resolution in the first place. In fact, *Time* magazine reports, "As many as 80% of people fail to keep their New Year's resolutions by February. Only 8% of people stick with them the entire year."[39] Why do so many people give up on their resolutions so quickly? Because we try to keep them by sheer willpower, believing that behavior change is all we need. But behavior change does not equal heart change.

We will never shame, guilt, and persuade ourselves into loving our bodies. No amount of dieting, exercising, or eliminating food groups will make us accept ourselves. If we simply change our behavior but continue to loathe ourselves, at our core we still believe the narrative that our worth is tied to our appearance. Behavior change fails because it is often built on a foundation of self-hatred.

It neglects to address and correct the lies we believe about ourselves, about our bodies. Heart change is what we're after—lasting, freeing heart change that tells us our bodies are good now, and they will be good in the future.

Of course, heart change isn't as quick a fix as behavior change can be. It won't give us an instant surge of pride like not eating sugar for a week might, but it will improve our self-image much more than shedding a few pounds. Heart change means delving into what we truly think about ourselves, about our bodies. It means addressing those falsehoods and replacing them with the truths of Scripture. It means refusing to treat our bodies as if they are disposable, unwanted, or unloved. It means caring for our whole selves, built upon an unshakable foundation of our immense worth as those made in God's image.

EMBRACING WHOLENESS

Behavior change does not equal heart change. I commit to healing my relationship with my body at a heart level.

80

Rushing Your Healing

The LORD is the one who will go before you. He
will be with you; he will not leave you or abandon
you. Do not be afraid or discouraged.

DEUTERONOMY 31:8 CSB

Our body, in all its complexity and beauty, holds the story of our life. It is a temple of our unique experiences, our deepest sorrows, and our greatest joys. In our eagerness to know and respect our body, we often fall into the trap of comparing our progress to others, forgetting that we cannot hurry toward healing. Today's verse reminds us that, in our complex journey with our own body, we can take our time, knowing God is with us through every emotion, setback, and breakthrough. God wants to provide you with deep healing in your relationship with your body, not provide you with a temporary motivator based on comparison.

When we compare our lived experience as embodied individuals with someone else's, we often find ourselves trying to rush healing. When we see that this friend loves their body and that neighbor exhibits shocking confidence in their everyday life, we reflect on our own journey and feel like we are falling short. Because we want to experience what it's like to relate to our bodies in the kinder, gentler way we see modeled in others, we try to ignore our complicated feelings in order to find an easy way to access that much sought-after freedom. But this type of progress only serves to cover up our deep wounds and hurts, making any peace we find with ourselves temporary. Because the catalyst for our healing is based in comparison with others, this healing is fleeting.

God is not concerned about a timeline, nor has He ever been. The Lord wants you to learn to appreciate, respect, and maybe even love your body because it was created by Him and in His image. Because He is God, He knows it may take months, years, or even a lifetime for you to find peace with your body. God isn't rushing your healing. He wants you to experience deep, lasting, life-changing growth in how to relate to and care for your body. And He promises to be with you, every step of the way.

EMBRACING WHOLENESS

I do not need to compare my healing journey to others or rush my progress. I can take my time as I discover how to have a healing relationship with my body.

81

Comfortable in Your Skin

Dear friend, I hope all is well with you and that you
are as healthy in body as you are strong in spirit.

3 JOHN 2:2

A big part of building trust with your body is learning how to be comfortable with the body you have today. Many of us try to ignore the fact that we are embodied people, finding it easier to disassociate from our physical form than to confront the more complicated emotions concerning our bodies. While this may seem like the better solution, we will never accept our bodies, and never fully experience the joy and holiness of being a part of the creation made in the image of God, if we spend our years ignoring them. When we acknowledge our bodies and work on being more comfortable in our skin, we take steps toward self-love while affirming that we are His creation, created "very good" just as we are (Genesis 1:31).

> **From birth, an integral part of what makes you *you* is your body.**

You are not a soul separated from a physical form while you are here on earth. From birth, an integral part of what makes you *you* is your body. When we recognize this, we can shift our perspective to see the ways we tend to our body every day as acts of compassion instead of annoying maintenance. For example, we fuel our bodies as an act of recognition—focusing on eating foods that both give us energy and allow ourselves to enjoy food as celebration, in community, or as comfort. We sleep and rest for our bodies to repair themselves, accepting that we are finite, embodied beings who cannot do it all. Even showering, brushing your teeth, or doing your hair tells your body that you are taking time to care and to keep yourself healthy.

When we acknowledge our bodies as we care for them, we naturally learn to appreciate our bodies more. You are already caring for your body through daily acts like sleeping, getting ready, eating, moving. At the same time, building a greater level of comfort with yourself could look like trying a new exercise, wearing something outside of your normal style, or taking a nap when you need it. These acts of care help us to trust and love our bodies more deeply. Working toward being more comfortable in your skin is a radical act, one that God will partner with you every step of the way.

EMBRACING WHOLENESS

I am an embodied person, and that matters. I will take care of my body's needs today, knowing that God sees my body as good.

82

On Personal Style

Now you are the body of Christ, and individual members of it.

1 CORINTHIANS 12:27 CSB

Gabrielle "Coco" Chanel is credited as having once said: "You were born an original, don't become a copy!"[40] And she's right; trends come and go, but what we like is innate to our very being. We are each drawn to different clothing, hairstyles, or makeup choices. Some like a preppy look with minimal makeup; some sport bright, bold colors and creative hairstyles; some enjoy following the ever-changing trends. Personal style is not only what we like and feel most ourselves in; it is an act of personal expression. Your style—the way you present yourself to the world—displays the complex beauty of our Creator. He created you with this innate understanding of what you feel like *you* in.

As today's passage explains, if you are a believer, you are part of the body of Christ. But it doesn't stop there—you are not only a member of a larger community; you are also an individual. Your individuality matters to God. When it comes to our relationship with our body: how we dress, do our makeup, and style our hair all relate to our understanding of our own self-worth and confidence. God could have created us to all be drawn to the same things, to reflect His image in identical ways. Instead, He purposed that we would be uniquely drawn to different colors, patterns, and styles as a way to reflect ourselves to the world. This is confirmation that we can brush off any shame and any pressure to fit in, and instead embrace and explore our personal style as evidence that we are each distinctive creations of God.

Even if you don't feel like you have a clear idea of what your style is, this is an opportunity for you to explore! Have you always wanted a dress like the one in your favorite movie? Maybe you've thought about getting a short haircut for years but have been worried about what someone's reaction will be. Or have you wanted to try a new makeup technique but felt ill-equipped? There is no shame in trying out different styles, being a beginner with hair or makeup, or thrifting instead of buying new. Your individuality matters, and you have the freedom to discover what style makes you feel like you.

EMBRACING WHOLENESS

God created me as an individual with my own sense of style. I can explore and embrace my personal style, all the while reflecting the unique image of God within me.

83

Fighting Classism

You should know this, Timothy, that in the last days
there will be very difficult times. For people will love
only themselves and their money. They will be boastful
and proud, scoffing at God, disobedient to their parents,
and ungrateful. They will consider nothing sacred.

2 TIMOTHY 3:1–2

Classism is defined as "a belief that a person's social or economic station in society determines their value in that society."[41] Classism is incompatible with the idea of humanity as the imago Dei (image of God) because it assigns worth to people based on the amount of money and power they possess. Even subtle beliefs or behaviors that reinforce a classist mindset harm the potential for unity and love for all people to share as God's creation.

The basis of modern classism is rooted in the judgment of others. We see someone who has more material possessions than we do, and we make assumptions about their life. They go on vacations, always have new clothes, and post pictures at fancy restaurants. Their life appears easier, more comfortable, and maybe even happier. On the opposite side of the spectrum, we compare ourselves to someone with less than us—economically or socially—to give ourselves a prideful boost. They don't have a group of close friends like we do, they haven't bought their own house, or they often post about couponing and thrift shopping. When we allow these forms of a classist mindset to overtake us, we are gauging how effectively we can compare ourselves to others to either tear them down or affirm the lack we find within ourselves. This isn't how God intended for us to live. God stated over and over again throughout Scripture the importance of unity among His people, of loving others without seeing them through the lens of social status and wealth (see Galatians 2:28; Proverbs 28:6; Mark 12:31).

God revealed to us that we will be tempted by the fleeting power that money and social status promise. But, with His love fueling us, we can fight this pervasive classist mindset and instead see each other as His beloved creations. We lead with love, knowing that everyone we encounter reflects His image in a unique way.

EMBRACING WHOLENESS

I commit to dismantling classism, recognizing instead the inherent worth and equality of all people.

84

Fighting Sexism

There is no longer Jew or Gentile, slave or free, male and female. For you are all one in Christ Jesus.

GALATIANS 3:28

Most of us have encountered sexism. Whatever we are doing—whether running errands, encountering competitive situations, or even inhabiting our own homes—people make assumptions about us based on our gender. *Merriam-Webster* defines sexism as "behavior, conditions, or attitudes that foster stereotypes of social roles based on sex."[42] From receiving unsolicited comments about your body, to being asked about marriage or children, to being reprimanded for being "bossy" at work when your male counterpart is applauded for being "assertive," sexism often asserts itself in subtly cutting ways. The ways you dress, speak, and relate to others are subjected to the double standard of sexism. It manifests itself in the form of unequal opportunities, gender-based violence, and harmful, often culturally accepted stereotypes. Sexism is a persistent force that seeks to diminish your value and potential based solely on your gender. This isn't okay. While this may seem obvious, sexism does not reflect the heart of God.

Our Creator intentionally designed both men and women, bestowing on each unique qualities and gifts that we can use for His glory in community. But when sexism takes root, it not only strips us of our dignity; it distorts God's plan for unity among His people. We can fight sexism by boldly calling out this injustice when we experience it, not only because it tarnishes the image of God within us but because it hinders the flourishing of His people here on earth. When we recognize sexism for what it is—inappropriate and harmful—we create opportunities for growth and for flourishing relationships.

Sexism is wrong. Let's actively challenge attitudes that belittle or dismiss others based on their gender and instead celebrate and empower one another's God-given potential. Let's actively pursue the liberating and affirming message of the gospel together, as reflected in today's verse, that we are unified under the banner of Christ. In Christ, all barriers are broken, and we stand as equals reflecting His image.

EMBRACING WHOLENESS

I am committed to demolishing sexism and upholding the inherent worth and equality of all, reflecting God's heart for His people. I can be bold in calling out sexism when I see and experience it, knowing God is with me and will empower me for the task.

85

Fighting Racism

For the LORD your God is God of gods and Lord
of lords, the great God, mighty and awesome, who
shows no partiality and accepts no bribes.

DEUTERONOMY 10:17 NIV

Racism of any kind stands in direct contradiction to the truth that all humankind is created in the image of God. To look at someone and see the image of God in them is to know their inherent worth as one whom God loves. To look at someone and judge them or make assumptions about them based on their race is to justify your own incorrect bias. Racism is "a belief that race is a fundamental determinant of human traits and capacities and that racial differences produce an inherent superiority of a particular race."[43] When we are bold enough to recognize and process through our own personal biases and fight racism in the broader culture, we help to move our community toward one that more accurately reflects the beauty in the diversity of God's creation.

Today's passage affirms that God shows no partiality and did not create any inherent superiority from human being to human being. Racism thrives on the illusion of supremacy, convincing us that some are worthier than others based solely on the color of their skin. Jesus fundamentally departs from this mindset, crossing cultural and societal boundaries to show us how to love one another well. It is time for us to emulate His example, actively fighting against the injustice of racism in all its forms.

Our path toward healing begins with recognition, acknowledging the presence of racism, however subtle or overt, in our heart and societies. Only when we work through our own inherent biases, privilege, or experience can we partner with God to refuse to be complicit in racism's perpetuation. We can challenge our own biases by seeking to understand and appreciate the experiences of those who are different from us. Engaging in open conversations, listening to diverse perspectives, and learning from the histories of marginalized people are good ways to start. When we fight racism first from within, we can join the many diverse voices already engaged in the broader fight, helping our world to be a more loving and beautiful place for all.

EMBRACING WHOLENESS

I commit to confronting racism both in my own life and in my community. I want everyone to experience the freeing truth that they are made in the image of God.

86

Releasing Your Ideal

Not that I have already reached the goal or am already perfect, but I make every effort to take hold of it because I also have been taken hold of by Christ Jesus. Brothers and sisters, I do not consider myself to have taken hold of it. But one thing I do: Forgetting what is behind and reaching forward to what is ahead, I pursue as my goal the prize promised by God's heavenly call in Christ Jesus.

PHILIPPIANS 3:12–14 csb

We all have an ideal body in our mind: one we dreamed about, dieted toward, and decided will make us happy, healthy, and whole. But as you progress toward body acceptance—seeing your body as "very good" because it is made in God's image (Genesis 1:31)—you can release that unreachable standard of a perfect body. God has not asked you to meet some unattainable or even unhealthy body standard, but instead asks you to pursue Him. In this holy pursuit, we can shift our focus from obsessing over an impossible body ideal to living a healthy and fulfilling life.

This healthy and fulfilling life looks different for each of us. True health encompasses not only our physical well-being but also our mental, emotional, and spiritual wholeness. As you learn to listen to your own body, take comfort in the fact that you don't have to determine what this new life means for you alone. There is no set of rules or regulations waiting to bring you down as is so often the case when you chase a perfect body. Instead, we discover what a healthy and fulfilling life looks like for us when we walk closely with God.

Or, as today's passage states in verse 12 (csB), Christ has "taken hold" of us, working within us as we pursue a life of wholeness.

Prayer is the biggest way we can develop a trusting relationship with God, discovering alongside Him what this healthy and fulfilling life means for each of us. You can treat your prayer life like an ongoing conversation, asking Him to help you gain freedom from diet culture and embrace your body and your life now. You can also nourish yourself with God's Word, feeding your soul with words of love, forgiveness, and gratitude. We can make intentional choices that honor our body, mind, and spirit as we release perfectionism and look toward fulfillment in Christ alone.

EMBRACING WHOLENESS

The impossible ideals I have set for my body and myself will not bring me meaning. Instead, I choose to release those fruitless standards and look to God to define what a healthy and rewarding life means to me.

87

Rerouting Your Energy

> And what do you benefit if you gain the whole world but lose
> your own soul? Is anything worth more than your soul?
>
> MATTHEW 16:26

Self-conscious and self-defeating thoughts steal a lot of our time and energy. You research new workout routines late into the night, plan out a restrictive diet for hours, or go through your clothes only to find nothing you feel comfortable in, leaving you frustrated and defeated. Most of us have lost hours upon hours to endeavors like these, all motivated by feelings of body dissatisfaction. Experiences like these prohibit you from making progress toward body acceptance. Each new diet or workout routine promises to make you feel better than ever but leaves you just as uncomfortable in your skin as you were before. Unrealistic body standards will take your time, your money, and your energy. They will keep you blaming yourself when you fail. It's time to take back and reroute that energy you've given to body shame and dieting. Your energy is precious, so why spend it in ways that will only discourage and dissatisfy you?

Part of the problem is we think that spending all this time, money, and energy to improve our body will make us skinnier, fitter, and happier. Instead, diet culture always asks more of us—trends change, diets come and go, and new exercise routines release. As today's verse explains, the more energy we put into this fleeting pursuit of measuring up to worldly standards, the more we lose ourselves in the end. As you work toward accepting your body as it is today—a beautiful creation made in the image of God—you also have the opportunity to leave this fleeting pursuit of perfection behind, rerouting all that energy to something more enjoyable, more life-giving, more you.

Diet culture tries to define beauty for us, morphing us into one homogeneous mass that looks the same. As you reclaim your uniqueness and recognize your body not as a project but as your home, you may be asking yourself, *Wait, what do I really enjoy?* Without the strict diet plan, the rigorous exercise, the obsession over calories, macros, or celery juice, who are you?

Maybe you're a knitter, a reader, or a cook. Maybe you discover you really do like running, because it makes you feel good, not because you hate your body. Maybe you find you want to take more naps, start volunteering at a homeless shelter, take more family hikes, or join a pottery class. As you come back to yourself, back to your body, take time to discover what you really want to devote your energy to. Come home to yourself, rejecting diet culture and finding out what truly brings you joy.

EMBRACING WHOLENESS

Striving to conform to unrealistic body standards and cultural beauty ideals isn't worth my energy. I can reroute this energy into life-giving hobbies that remind me that my body is good.

88

Information Curation

But test all things. Hold on to what is good.

1 THESSALONIANS 5:21 CSB

Healing your relationship with your body is a process toward progress, continually releasing societal pressures, diet culture ideals, and your own warped self-image. While much of this work happens internally, you cannot discount outside factors that impact your view of your body. For example, you can pray, journal, and speak more kindly to yourself, but if you are watching shows that make you hate your body, following accounts on social media that reinforce unhealthy body standards, and reading books or listening to podcasts that only affirm your deepest insecurities, progress toward self-love will be more arduous and discouraging. Part of acknowledging, respecting, and loving yourself is curating the information you allow into your mind about self-image and bodies.

Putting up boundaries around the content you engage in can be incredibly helpful as part of your body-acceptance journey. You can do so nonjudgmentally, knowing that what may not trigger or harm someone else does impact you negatively, so it is totally okay to do away with it. As you walk through each day consuming all manner of media—from books to television to social media—notice what type of content makes you feel self-conscious, insecure, or as if you're not enough. Give yourself permission to unfollow or mute those on social media that don't aid your mission to love yourself. It's nothing against them, but it is actively hurting you. Instead, follow accounts that enthusiastically promote self-love and help you grow emotionally, spiritually, and mentally. Allow yourself to stop watching shows that pinpoint your fears about your appearance or reading books that make you feel like you are less than. Even if you once loved that reality dating show or that celebrity podcast, try taking a three- to six-month break from it. You can always come back to it, but it's not benefiting your healing right now. Instead, look up podcasts or books that discuss body acceptance, or watch shows that feature characters of all sizes, shapes, and colors. There are plenty out there that will encourage and affirm you as they spur you on toward loving yourself.

You have an opportunity here to practice discernment, looking internally to determine what nourishes you. If you are unsure, the Holy Spirit is incredibly discerning and is there to help you at all times. You can pray to Him, asking for clarity and boldness. As 1 Corinthians 14:33 (ESV) says, "God is not a God of confusion but of peace." Curating the content you allow into your life will only benefit you in your self-love journey.

EMBRACING WHOLENESS

I have the power to decide what type of media and messaging I consume.

89

A Life that Pleases God

Finally, dear brothers and sisters, we urge you
in the name of the Lord Jesus to live in a way
that pleases God, as we have taught you.

1 THESSALONIANS 4:1

To live a life that pleases our Creator is not a onetime goal but a continuous journey, one that is surprisingly interconnected with our body. While it may seem intimidating to try to "live in a way that pleases God" (1 Thessalonians 4:1), the Bible serves as our roadmap for this adventure called being a human. It involves a deliberate and continuous effort to align ourselves with our Creator, seeking to follow His plan. But we do not have to strive to please God in our own strength, but through the motivation and power that He provides us. To mindfully commit to live out our days in ways that honor God is to move toward a holy, peaceful, and free life.

What does this mean practically? To work to honor God with our lives is to resist the distractions, temptations, and pressures of this world. Paul explains in 1 Thessalonians 4:3–4 that this includes staying away from sexual sin because it causes us to lose control of our bodies, living for our passions instead of for our God (see Ephesians 5). As 1 Thessalonians 4:7 explains, "God has called us to live holy lives, not impure lives." This desire to please God with our lives also includes resisting harming or cheating one another, but instead living a quiet life "minding your own business" (1 Thessalonians 4:11).

God is not asking for perfection here or standing ready to judge you when you hurt someone or make a mistake. Instead, He desires your continual movement toward Him, not away from Him. As 1 Corinthians 6:20 explains, God wants you to respect Him with your body, and He rejoices when you experience freedom from body shame. There is no condemnation here for those who are in Christ Jesus (Romans 8:1), only an instruction manual that will provide you with greater peace in this life and hope for eternity in heaven with God. Living a life that pleases God means aligning your thoughts, actions, and attitude with His. It means caring for your body well because it is His creation, made in His image. It means following His Word—the Bible—and seeking to honor Him each day.

EMBRACING WHOLENESS

My desire is to please God with my body and my life, not only by avoiding sinful behaviors but also by cultivating a life and a relationship with my body that brings glory to His name. I will seek to make choices that align with my identity as a beloved child of God.

God rejoices when
you experience
freedom from
body shame.

90

Good News

For God so loved the world that he gave his one and only
Son, that whoever believes in him shall not perish but have
eternal life. For God did not send his Son into the world to
condemn the world, but to save the world through him.

JOHN 3:16–17 NIV

We have a lot to work through when it comes to our relationship with our body. Many of us carry shame, blame, and trauma. Add the heavy weights of cultural messaging, diet culture, and beauty standards, and the load is oppressive, too much for us to handle. But we don't ever have to bear it alone, for we have a Savior who came down from heaven, was born in a physical body as a baby, and then sacrificed His body on the cross for us. Jesus did this for you, so you could have a relationship with God. God is always there for you, ready to carry your burdens and usher you toward healing. Through Him, you can experience freedom from body shame and can walk in confidence. You are loved and worthy of love. You are created in the image of a holy, loving, and creative God.

God wants to have a relationship with you because He loves you more than you can imagine. You were created in His image, and you will find abundant life in Him alone. You are never too broken, too lost, or too complicated for God. The good news of Jesus is for you, and if you don't have a personal relationship with Him, today could be your day. Whether you feel at home in the body God created just for you or you are still grappling with insecurity and low self-esteem,

Jesus loves you and wants to be near to you. Psalm 145:18 (NIV) says: "The LORD is near to all who call on him, to all who call on him in truth."

If you have yet to give your life over to the Healer, know that He is ready to welcome you with open arms. God's love for you is immeasurable and unconditional. It's a love that surpasses all human understanding—a love that doesn't depend on our worthiness or our actions but is freely given to us. We will only find true peace and healing in our relationship with our bodies when we root ourselves in the good news of the gospel of Jesus Christ.

EMBRACING WHOLENESS

I am deeply loved by my Creator, and through Jesus, I have the gift of eternal life.

Glossary of Terms

- **Anti-Diet:** Anti-diet refers to a movement that focuses on the health of your whole self—body, mind, soul. God created you to be in a life-giving relationship with Him, and self-imposed restrictive diets steal your attention away from and rob you of the loving relationship with both God and your body. Key Scripture: 1 Corinthians 6:12

- **Body Acceptance:** Body acceptance means working to accept yourself—your physical body and your appearance—as you are right now. We still live in a fallen world, and sin affects our bodies through circumstances and our own choices. But for Christians, this acceptance is grounded in the truth that your body was crafted intentionally by God, and He has a plan to redeem your whole being one day. He accepts you and your body today—because He knew what your body would look like and purposefully, lovingly created you this way. Key Scripture: Psalm 139:13–14

- **Body Positivity:** Body positivity takes body acceptance one step further, asserting that you can not only accept but can also love your whole self, including your physical body. A Christian view of body positivity is rooted in the truth that God created and loved your body, calling it "very good" (Genesis 1:31). Your body is worthy of positivity because it was made in the image of God and reflects His goodness. Key Scripture: Genesis 1:27

- **Body Respect:** Body respect is a part of body acceptance and body positivity. It is the overflow of viewing your body as an intentional, purposeful creation of God, crafted to reflect His character in unique ways. Practically, body respect means treating yourself—physically, emotionally, spiritually, mentally—with the respect one who is made in God's image deserves. Key Scripture: 1 Corinthians 6:19–20

- **Diet Culture:** Diet culture refers to a societal belief that thinness and conventional attractiveness are the highest values, above all else. It equates thinness and attractiveness with morality. The Bible tells us that the Lord looks at our heart, that loving others is Jesus's second greatest commandment behind loving God (Matthew 22:36–40). Key Scripture: 1 Samuel 16:7

- **Self-Acceptance:** Similar to body acceptance, self-acceptance encompasses an acceptance of your whole being, as God created you to be. Although we are broken by sin, we can accept the redeeming power of God at work in us. Often the precursor to self-love, a Christian viewpoint of self-acceptance reminds us that God accepts us as we are. We are sinners in need of His grace, and He loves us here and now. Key Scripture: Philippians 1:6

- **Self-Love:** The foundation of self-love from a Christian perspective lies in the truth that you are created in the image of God, and you are defined by His unending love and grace toward you. His love is so great that loving yourself delights God, as He sees that you understand how He feels about you. He loves you so much that He is honored when you love yourself, even as you are growing and changing throughout your life. Key Scripture: 1 John 4:19

Notes

1. Adapted with permission from my previously published article "Made in His Image," *Everyday Faith Magazine* (DaySpring), summer 2024, 66.

2. Francis A. Schaeffer, *Escape from Reason* (Downers Grove, IL: InterVarsity Press, 2014), 32–33.

3. Crescent B. Martin, et. al., "Attempts to Lose Weight Among Adults in the United States, 2013–2016," NCHS Data Brief, no. 313 (2018), National Center for Health Statistics, last modified July 12, 2018, https://www.cdc.gov/nchs/products/databriefs/db313.htm.

4. Janet Polivy, "Psychological Consequences of Food Restriction" Journal of the Academy of Nutrition and Dietetics 96, no. 2 (1996): abstract, https://www.jandonline.org/article/S0002-8223(96)00161-7/fulltext.

5. "Strength," *Merriam-Webster*, accessed December 17, 2024, https://www.merriam-webster.com/dictionary/strength.

6. Leigh Campbell, "We've Broken Down Your Entire Life Into Years Spent Doing Tasks," *Huffpost*, October 18, 2017, https://www.huffpost.com/entry/weve-broken-down-your-entire-life-into-years-spent-doing-tasks_n_61087617e4b0999d2084fec5.

7. Adapted with permission from my previously published article "Made in His Image," *Everyday Faith Magazine* (DaySpring), summer 2024, 66.

8. Adapted with permission from my previously published article "Discovering the Holy Spirit," *Everyday Faith Magazine* (DaySpring), summer 2024, 35.

9. Meryl Davids Landau, "Rethinking Fatness: Why Everything You've Been Told about Weight May Be Wrong," *Prevention*, April 14, 2021, https://www.prevention.com/weight-loss/a36065492/rethinking-body-weight/.

10. Linda Bacon, *Health at Every Size: The Surprising Truth About Your Weight* (Dallas, TX: BenBella Books, 2010), 258.

11. Kristin Neff, "Definition and Three Elements of Self Compassion," *Self*, July 9, 2020, https://self-compassion.org/the-three-elements-of-self-compassion-2/.

12. "Advocate," *Merriam-Webster*, accessed July 31, 2023, https://www.merriam-webster.com/dictionary/advocate.

13. Christine Batchelder, "10 Quotes from Billy Graham on Service," The Billy Graham Library, last modified November 10, 2021, https://billygrahamlibrary.org/blog-10-quotes-from-billy-graham-on-service/.

14. "Skin," Cleveland Clinic, accessed June 27, 2024, https://my.clevelandclinic.org/health/body/10978-skin.

15. "Brain Health [from Healthy Brains]," Cleveland Clinic, May 11, 2020, https://healthybrains.org/brain-facts/.

16. Michael Miller, "7 Amazing Facts about Emotions," *Six Seconds*, February 15, 2023, https://www.6seconds.org/2022/08/19/7-amazing-facts-emotions/.

17. Wayne Grudem, "What Is the Soul? Is It Different from the Spirit?" Zondervan Academic, accessed August 29, 2024, https://zondervanacademic.com/blog/what-is-the-soul.

18. "Field Listing—World Biomes," Central Intelligence Agency, accessed August 29, 2024, https://www.cia.gov /the-world-factbook/field/world-biomes/.

19. "In Images: Plastic Is Forever," United Nations, accessed August 29, 2024, https://www.un.org/en/exhibits/exhibit /in-images-plastic-forever.

20. "Integrity," *Merriam-Webster*, accessed December 17, 2024, https://www.merriam-webster.com/dictionary/integrity.

21. Elisabeth Elliot, *Shadow of the Almighty* (Peabody, MA: Hendrickson Publishers, 2008), 121.

22. Dominique Petruzzie, "Size of the anti-aging market worldwide from 2021 to 2027," *Statista*, June 25, 2024, https://www.statista.com/statistics/509679/value-of -the-global-anti-aging-market/.

23. Article adapted with permission from my previously published article "Discovering the Holy Spirit," *Everyday Faith Magazine* (DaySpring), summer 2024, 35–37.

24. J. I. Packer, *God's Plans for You* (Wheaton, IL: Crossway, 2001), 154.

25. Max Knoblauch, "Americans Feel Guilty about Almost a Third of the Food They Eat," New York Post, March 13, 2019, https://nypost.com/2019/03/13/americans-feel -guilty-about-almost-a-third-of-the-food-they-eat/.

26. Diane L. Dunton, *Living, Learning, Healing: Inspirational Stories from the Heart* (Biddeford Pool, ME: Rainbow River Press, 2017), dedication.

27. Jon Simpson, "Finding Brand Success in the Digital World," *Forbes*, October 12, 2022, https://www.forbes.com/sites /forbesagencycouncil/2017/08/25/finding-brand-success -in-the-digital-world/?sh=577869a8626e.

28. "How to Find Joy in Exercise," Kendall Reagan Nutrition Center, accessed January 5, 2022, https://www.chhs .colostate.edu/krnc/monthly-blog/how-to-find-joy-in -exercise.

29. "Mental Health," World Health Organization, accessed August 1, 2023, https://www.who.int/news-room/fact -sheets/detail/mental-health-strengthening-our-response.

30. Taylor Andrews and Hannah Chubb, "40 Inspirational Mental Health Quotes to Read When You Have a Bad Day," accessed August 1, 2023, https://www.cosmopolitan.com /health-fitness/a34363089/mental-health-quotes/.

31. "Children, Teens, Media, and Body Image," infographic, Common Sense Media, accessed December 16, 2024, https://www.commonsensemedia.org/children-teens -body-image-media-infographic.

32. Raisa Bruner, "Blake Lively Says '99.9%' of Celeb Images Are Photoshopped While Interviewing Gigi Hadid," *Time*, April 11, 2018, https://time.com/5236384/blake-lively -photoshop-gigi-hadid-interview/.

33. Tonya Freyert and Lisa Walker, "Physical Attractiveness and Social Status," *Sociology Compass* 8, no. 3 (2014): 313–323, https://www.researchgate.net/publication /260911923_Physical_Attractiveness_and_Social_Status.

34. David G. Benner, *The Gift of Being Yourself: The Sacred Call to Self-Discovery* (Downers Grove, IL: IVP Books, 2015), 46.

35. Mark Buchanan, *The Rest of God: Restoring Your Soul by Restoring Sabbath* (Nashville, TN: Thomas Nelson, 2007), 3.

36. Jill Waggoner, "Why We Need a Biblical Understanding of 'Self-Care,'" The Ethics and Religious Liberty Commission, last modified June 27, 2022, https://erlc.com/resource/why-we-need-a-biblical-understanding-of-self-care/.

37. "Hospitality," Dictionary.com, accessed August 9, 2023, https://www.dictionary.com/browse/hospitality.

38. "9 Notable Quotes from the Gospel Comes with a House Key," *Crossway*, May 22, 2020, https://www.crossway.org/articles/9-notable-quotes-from-the-gospel-comes-with-a-house-key/.

39. Jay Van Bavel and Dominic Packer, "How Not to Fail at Keeping Your New Year's Resolutions," *Time*, December 29, 2022, https://time.com/6243642/how-to-keep-new-years-resolutions-2/.

40. "Coco Chanel: Top 10 Inspirational Quotes for Women of Today!," Pairfum London, accessed December 17, 2024, https://www.pairfum.com/coco-chanels-top-10-inspirational-quotes-for-women-of-today/.

41. "Classism," *Merriam-Webster*, accessed August 17, 2023, https://www.merriam-webster.com/dictionary/classism.

42. "Sexism," *Merriam-Webster*, accessed August 17, 2023, https://www.merriam-webster.com/dictionary/sexism.

43. "Racism," *Merriam-Webster*, accessed August 21, 2023, https://www.merriam-webster.com/dictionary/racism.

GOD HEARS HER

Seek and she will find

Spread the Word
by Doing One Thing.

- Give a copy of this book as a gift.
- Share the QR code link via your social media.
- Write a review of this book on your blog, favorite bookseller's website, or at ourdailybreadpublishing.org.
- Recommend this book to your church, small group, or book club.

Connect with us. 🇫 📷

Our Daily Bread Publishing
PO Box 3566, Grand Rapids, MI 49501, USA
Email: books@odbm.org

Love God. Love Others.
with  Our Daily Bread®

Your gift changes lives.

Connect with us. 𝕗 ⊙

Our Daily Bread Publishing
PO Box 3566, Grand Rapids, MI 49501, USA
Email: books@odbm.org